LABORATORY STUDIES

IN

ELEMENTARY CHEMISTRY

BY

LeROY C. COOLEY, Ph.D.

PROFESSOR OF PHYSICS AND CHEMISTRY IN VASSAR COLLEGE

NEW YORK ∴ CINCINNATI ∴ CHICAGO

AMERICAN BOOK COMPANY

In order to secure these results, no desultory or haphazard work should be tolerated in the laboratory.

Every experiment should be undertaken with a well-defined object in view. Every step in the work should be taken in accordance with a deliberately formed plan.

The beginner will need the help of the most specific directions for work, and considerable prompting toward the observation of results. He will also need sympathetic encouragement to describe what he actually sees, and constant attention, lest he record his observation in bad form.

On the other hand, his mind should not be prejudiced by foreknowledge of the facts which the experiments are competent to reveal, for the beginner finds it very difficult not to see that which he knows ought to be seen. That his observations may be genuine, he should not be subjected to the temptation or unconscious tendency to twist the statement of what is actually seen into the statement of what the text-book says should appear. This may be avoided by giving very specific directions for the work, so that the right conditions shall be secured in the experiment, and then leaving the results to be detected by the student, and stated in his own words. The laboratory guide and the general text-book should therefore be separate volumes.

But experimental work is not all there should be in the school or college course; along with the specific discipline of such work there should be the broadening influence of a text-book, or course of lectures. The laboratory and the classroom should work hand in hand.

The following course of laboratory studies is constructed in accordance with the foregoing views of what should be the aims of experimental chemistry in the general educational work of the schools.

A wise selection of laboratory studies devoted to fundamental facts and principles will furnish satisfactory materials for use in connection with any course in elementary general chemistry which the teacher may choose to use. The number of experiments may be larger than are needed; the order in which they are placed may not be the order chosen for the discussion of the subjects to which they relate; but the independent teacher will find that their value is not lessened by the need of selection.

I believe that the subjects treated in this book are such as should be chosen for the purpose stated. I am quite sure that the order in which they are given is a logical order, but I believe that it is not the only one. I would leave the teacher, who desires to do so, quite free to map out the lecture or text-book course for himself, but would furnish a stock of materials which may be drawn upon for the laboratory part of it, in any course, provided only that it is devoted to elementary general chemistry.

In conclusion I may gratefully add that I am indebted to Miss E. M. FREEMAN and to PROFESSOR C. W. MOULTON for valuable suggestions in regard to details in several of the " Studies " in this course.

L. C. C.

VASSAR COLLEGE, January, 1894.

SUGGESTIONS TO THE STUDENT.

IN REGARD TO THE WORK. — In each study proceed in the following order : —

1. Notice the object of the experiment, and read the directions for the work which is to accomplish it.

2. Arrange the apparatus and use it exactly as directed. Do not attempt modifications until your experience in manipulation is large enough to warrant your doing so.

3. Watch intently for every change that takes place, and note accurately every important change as soon as it has occurred.

4. Study the results thoughtfully in order to detect their meaning and discover what they teach.

5. Compare the results with others which you may have obtained with other substances under similar conditions, and try to discover the differences and the resemblances of the properties and actions of the substances involved.

IN REGARD TO NOTES. — The notebook should be always at hand, and you should heroically insist on making the notes of your experiment *at the time*, while the experiment is going on.

Notes should be the *original record* of the work : no copies of them should be offered to, or accepted by, the instructor.

7

After they have been examined by the instructor, and the corrections made, they may be copied into your blank book for preservation, and used for reference and reviews.

In the notes on every experiment you should —

1. Briefly describe the apparatus and materials used, their arrangement and the work done with them. A simple sketch of the apparatus is very useful.

2. Briefly describe all the changes that occur during the operations.

3. Briefly state the conclusions drawn, or give an explanation of the changes, and show what the experiment teaches.

CONTENTS.

PART I.

Chemistry of Nonmetals.

PART II.

Reactions and Properties of some Compounds of Metals. and Exercises in tabulating Results.

9

10   CONTENTS.

PART III.

Application of Certain Foregoing Reactions to Qualitative Analysis.

APPENDIX.

PART I.

CHEMISTRY OF NONMETALS.

I. CHEMICAL CHANGES.

EXPERIMENT 1.

Object. — *To ascertain the effect of heating magnesium.*

Manipulation. — Obtain a piece of magnesium wire or ribbon about six inches long; grasp one end of it with pincers, and hold the other end for a few moments in the flame of the Bunsen lamp and then over a sheet of paper on the table while the change goes on.

Notes. — Describe the work, as you did it, briefly in your own words. Describe all the changes you can discover. Note particularly whether the substance of the wire or ribbon is changed.

EXPERIMENT 2.

Object. — *To ascertain the effect of heating iron.*

Manipulation. — Use a piece of iron wire, and proceed to heat it as you heated the magnesium in Exp. 1.

Notes. — Briefly describe the work in your own words. Describe all the changes you can discover. Note particularly whether the substance of the wire is changed.

General. — In the foregoing experiments you should discover the marked difference in magnesium and iron with respect to *the changes* produced by heat in the *nature* of these substances. The change witnessed in magnesium is

11

typical of one kind of changes in bodies generally, known as *chemical changes;* while those seen in the iron are typical of the other kind, known as *physical changes.*

EXPERIMENT 3.

Object. — *To ascertain the effect of heat on mercuric oxide, and to distinguish the physical from the chemical changes.*

Manipulation. — Put 1 g. of mercuric oxide into a side-neck ignition tube [1] (Fig. 1). Close the mouth of the tube with a tightly fitting cork, and slip one end of a piece of rubber tubing (*e*, Fig. 2) over the end of the side neck, and the other over the end of a glass tube long enough to reach the bottom of the test tube, as shown. Fix the side-neck tube obliquely in a clamp of the retort stand *f.* Put 3 cc. of water into the test tube *b*, and the glass delivery tube into it.

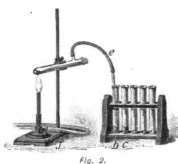

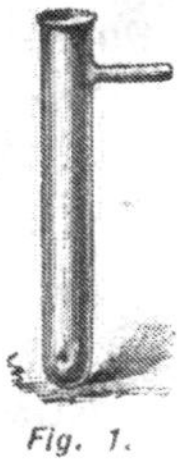

Fig. 1.

Fig. 2.

Apply the flame of a lamp, and move it slowly to heat the glass gradually and evenly, remembering that the upper part of the tube should not be heated (discover why farther

[1] The tube must be clean and dry. A piece of dry cloth, or a sponge tied on the end of a wire or stick, is convenient for wiping tubes. Ignition tubes are made of "hard" glass, while other tubes are made of "soft" glass. Hard glass will stand a strong heat, while soft glass will not. Common test tubes may be used for heating liquids; ignition tubes should be used for heating dry solids.

on). Watch for and note the changes as they occur. While bubbles are escaping rapidly in *b*, light a long splinter of wood; extinguish the flame; thrust the glowing end down into the tube.

Notes. — Describe all the changes. Note particularly every evidence of the production of two new substances, and of the loss of the mercuric oxide.

End the Experiment. — When the action has nearly ceased, or at any time you may wish to stop it, remove the glass tube from the water in *b ;* lower the gas flame to *cool the ignition tube gradually.* When the ignition tube can be handled, place it erect, and put the glowing end of a splinter into it. Try it again.

Notes. — Describe all changes which occur while the tube is cooling. Consider what substances have been brought out of the oxide by the heat.[1] What physical changes in the oxide occurred? What chemical changes? Why should the upper end of the ignition tube be kept cold in this experiment? Why should the ignition tube be cooled gradually?

EXPERIMENT 4.

Object. — *To ascertain the physical and chemical effects of heat on potassium chlorate.*

Manipulation. — Grind 2 g. of potassium chlorate in a mortar (Fig. 3). Transfer it to a *dry* ignition tube, arrange the apparatus as shown in Fig. 2, and proceed to study the effects of heat as directed in Exp. 3.

When the glowing end of the splinter shows that the air has been all driven out of tube *b*, transfer the delivery tube *e* over

Fig. 3.

---

[1] Oxygen is a colorless gas which intensifies combustion. Mercury is a lustrous, silver-colored, liquid metal.

into test tube *c*. Two or three test tubes may be filled with the gas in this way. Each one should be immediately closed with a cork.

Notes. — Describe all the changes seen in the chlorate. Note particularly every evidence of the production of new substances. Name that found in the test tubes. What physical changes did the heat produce in the chlorate? What chemical changes?

EXPERIMENT 5.

Object. — *To study the effect of oxygen on red-hot charcoal.*

Manipulation. — Wind the end of a small wire around a little splinter of charcoal. Heat the tip of the charcoal until it glows; then lower it into the gas in the test tube *c* (Fig. 2). Pour a little strong limewater into *c*; close the tube and shake it briskly. Add limewater to tube *b*; close it and shake briskly.

Notes. — Describe the action of oxygen on the hot charcoal; also the change in the limewater in *c*. Judge by the limewater in *b* whether the effect in *c* is caused by oxygen. How can you account for the change in the limewater?[1] Where now are the oxygen and the carbon (charcoal) which were used up in the action?

EXPERIMENT 6.

Object. — *To study the changes produced by the mutual action of the vapors of ammonia and hydrochloric acid.*

Manipulation. — Put about 1 cc. of ammonia water into a tube or bottle; rinse the walls with it, and pour the excess away. Put as much hydrochloric acid into another similar vessel, and treat it in the same way. By this means

---

[1] Carbon dioxide is a colorless gas which whitens limewater.

the vessels are filled with the colorless vapors of the two substances. Bring the two vessels mouth to mouth, and hold them one above the other (Fig. 4).

Notes. — Describe the chemical change. How can you account for the new substance?

General. — The change witnessed in Exps. 3 and 4 were alike in this respect: a single substance disappeared, while two others were obtained. These changes typify a large class of chemical changes, called *decomposition*. The changes in Exps. 5 and 6 were alike, but in marked contrast with the others in this respect: two substances disappeared, while one only was obtained. These changes are typical of another class of chemical changes, called *combination*.

Fig. 4.

EXPERIMENT 7.

Object. — *To study the changes produced by the mutual action of zinc and dilute sulphuric acid.*

Manipulation and Notes.[1] — Into a wide-mouthed bottle which can hold about 200 cc. put about 50 cc. of water, and add, little by little, 8 cc. of strong sulphuric acid, shaking the bottle meantime to mix the liquids. Note an important effect.[2] Drop fragments of zinc, about 10 g., into the dilute acid, and cover the bottle with a square of glass or of heavy paper (*note*).[3] Lift the cover, and at the same

---

[1] Since results should be described as soon as they are seen, you will find henceforth the hints for notes given with the directions for manipulation.

[2] This effect becomes dangerously great when water is poured into the acid. **This should never be done.** Whenever strong sulphuric acid and water are to be mixed, always *pour the acid* gradually *into the water* while you stir it.

[3] The word *note* will henceforth indicate that you should here discover results of special value, and describe them in your notes.

moment bring a match flame to the mouth of the bottle (*note*). Let the action go on until the effervescence (escape of gas bubbles) is quite or nearly ended. There may be a residue of zinc and also a black sediment in the liquid. This sediment is the impurity of the zinc which has disappeared. Can you detect any change in the dilute acid? It may, nevertheless, contain some new substance in solution.

To Search for a Product in Solution. — The liquid must be rid of any sediment. To obtain it clear, it should be *filtered ;* and then, to obtain any solid it may be holding in solution, it may be *evaporated.*

1. *Filtration.* — Cut a square of filter paper (*A*, Fig. 5), the length of one side being

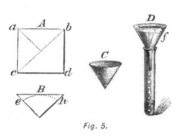

a little less than twice the length of the sloping side of a funnel, *D.* Fold the square into a triangle by bringing corners *d* and *a* together. Fold again, bringing corners *c* and *b* together, making the triangle *B.* Trim the edges along a circular line, *e B h.* Open the triangle (leaving three thicknesses of paper on one side, and one on the other), and you will have a little paper funnel, *C,* which will fit neatly in the glass funnel *D.* Press it into *D* and wet it with water. Then rest *D* on a test tube and pour the liquid into it. The clear liquid which should run through it is called a *filtrate.*

Fig. 5.

2. *Evaporation.* — Pour the clear liquid into an evaporating dish and heat it over a *low* flame, as shown in Fig. 6. *Evaporation is not boiling.* To evaporate a liquid, you may heat it until it begins to simmer, but should not agitate it by violent ebullition. This caution is especially needed when the volume of the liquid is small, and absolutely

necessary when no loss must be incurred. Evaporate this liquid until a drop, when cooled on a glass rod or plate, will yield a solid. Then let the liquid cool.

Describe the result, and compare any solid product with the substances used. How many and what are the products of the mutual action of zinc and sulphuric acid ? [1]

Fig. 6.

Compare the number of substances used with the number of new ones obtained, and judge whether the chemical change is a simple decomposition, or a direct combination, or neither.

EXPERIMENT 8.

Object. — *To study the changes produced by the mutual action of sodium chloride and silver nitrate in solution.*

Manipulation and Notes. — Drop a small crystal of silver nitrate into a test tube containing 5 cc. of water, and shake it until it is dissolved. In another tube dissolve a little sodium chloride (common salt). Add a drop or two of the chloride to the nitrate (*note*). Go on adding the solution of the chloride carefully, drop by drop, shaking the tube vigorously after each addition, and letting the upper layer of the liquid become clear enough to let you see whether the next drop makes any change. Do this until a drop makes no change, and then stir the liquid with a glass rod wet with the silver-nitrate solution. Your liquid can now contain almost none at all of either silver nitrate or sodium chloride unchanged.

---

[1] *Hydrogen* is a colorless gas which takes fire with explosion. *Zinc sulphate* is a solid which dissolves in water, but reappears, on evaporation, in the form of slender, colorless crystals.

2

Filter the mixture. Describe the precipitate (the solid left on the filter) when it is fresh, and again after it has been exposed to sunlight.

Evaporate the filtrate until little is left, and then let it cool quietly (*note*).

What are the products of the mutual action of silver nitrate and sodium chloride? [1] Judge whether the change is simple decomposition, or direct combination, or neither. Also see whether you can find any difference between this case and that in Exp. 7.

EXPERIMENT 9.

Object. — *To study the change produced by the mutual action of mercuric chloride and potassium iodide in solution.*

Manipulation and Notes. — Use enough mercuric chloride, in powder, to halfway fill the rounded part of the bottom of a test tube. Cover it with about 5 cc. of water, and warm it until it is dissolved. Put about twice as much potassium iodide into another tube, and dissolve it also in water. Pour about 150 cc. of water into a wide-mouthed bottle, and add the solution of mercuric chloride. Next add about half of the solution of potassium iodide little by little (*note*).

Go on adding the iodide carefully, noticing whether more of the new substance is made by each addition; and, that you need make no mistake, wait each time until the liquid clears before you add the next drop. Do this until the last drop yields no change; then stir the liquid with a glass rod wet with mercuric chloride (*give reason*).[2]

[1] Silver chloride is, when freshly made, easily darkened by exposure to light; and when dry, a white powder. Sodium nitrate is a solid, soluble in water, from which it crystallizes by evaporation.

[2] The words *give reason* or *explain* will henceforth be used to ask you to give a reason for, or make an explanatory statement in regard to, whatever subject is immediately before it. In this case it means, *Why* stir with a glass rod wet with mercuric chloride?

Filter the mixture and evaporate the filtrate (*note*). What are the products of the changes in this experiment? [1] Are the changes examples of simple decomposition, or of direct combination? Can you decide whether they are like those found in Exp. 7, or those in Exp. 8?

EXPERIMENT 10.

Object. — *To study the action of iron and sulphur in the cold, and when heated.*

Manipulation and Notes. — Mix 1.5 g. of the finest iron filings with .84 g. of flowers of sulphur very intimately in a mortar. Look at a little of this substance with a strong magnifying glass, to see if you can detect the grains of iron and of sulphur (*note*). Judge whether any chemical change has occurred.

Transfer the substance to an iron spoon, or an ignition tube, and heat it intensely, even to redness if necessary (*note*). Pulverize the product in a mortar, examine it closely, and judge whether a chemical change has occurred.

General. — Substances intimately mingled together, but retaining their properties, constitute a *mixture*. If substances lose their identity by mutual action when brought together, the product is a chemical *compound*.

---

[1] Mercuric iodide is a scarlet solid, insoluble in water. Potassium chloride is a white solid, soluble in water.

II. PREPARATION AND STUDY OF GASES.

I. To Liberate and Collect a Gas.

1. *Collecting by Displacement of Air.* — Use a set of flasks or bottles fitted up as shown in Figs. 7 and 8.   A conical flask is provided with a soft-rubber stopper with two holes. Through each hole there passes a glass tube bent at right angles, — one with a long branch to reach almost to the bottom of the flask, the other only long enough to reach through the

Fig. 7.

stopper.   You can easily cut these tubes to proper length with a triangular file, and bend them when softened by a Bunsen flame. As many of these collecting flasks as you may need can be joined in series, as shown in Fig. 8, — the long tube of *a* with the tube of the side-neck generator, and the long tube of each one following with the short tube of the one before it.   The ends of the glass tubes are joined by

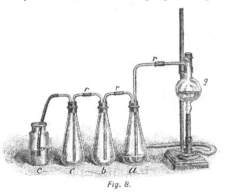

Fig. 8.

short pieces of rubber (*r, r*), and should meet inside these connections. From the last flask a rubber tube may reach over into water in an open bottle, *e*.

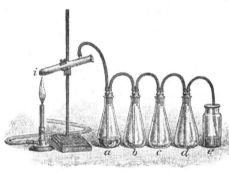

The gas may be "washed" by bubbling through water in *a ;* and another advantage of this water, and that in *e* also, is this : you can see by the bubbles whether the gas is coming off rapidly or slowly, and can regulate the heat accordingly.

Fig. 9

All the flasks *must be closed air-tight.* Rubber stoppers easily make air-tight joints.[1]

Instead of the "all-glass connection" just described, "rubber-tube connection" may be used, as shown in Fig. 10. The stopper of each flask is provided with straight glass tubes, as in Fig. 9, and the flasks are connected by pieces of rubber tubing six or eight inches long. The apparatus is more quickly and easily set up in this way, at first ; but glass is more reliable than rubber for conveying gases, and the set, once prepared with glass, can be as quickly put together afterward as the other.

Fig. 10.

All joints should be tested, *and proved to be air-tight,* by trying to force the breath through them.

[1] A set once fitted up is a sort of general gas works for the laboratory table; for, as we shall see, most gases may be collected in this way. To collect gases lighter than air, the flasks should be joined with their *short tubes toward the generator.*

2. *Collecting by Displacement of Water.* — The gas is led from the generator (*g*, Fig. 11) by a delivery tube (*t*) of glass or rubber, to the mouth of a bottle, cylinder, or flask, previously filled with water and inverted in a water pan or cistern (*B*). A piece of smooth tile

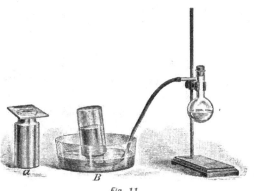

Fig. 11.

or marble, or some equivalent, about 2¼ inches square and ¼ inch thick, for the bottle to stand on, with the mouth projecting over its edge, is desirable, although one can do without it, as shown in the cut.

Small bottles or tubes may be filled with water by simple immersion in the pan, but the water must not be deep; hence proceed as follows. Fill the bottle to the brim with water. Cut a piece of paper a little larger than its mouth; *slide* it on as a cover, and smooth it down closely upon the glass (Fig. 11, *a*). Grasp the bottle, and turn it bottom upward over the pan; lower it into the water; remove the paper, and leave the bottle standing in the water. The pressure of the atmosphere will safely hold the water in the bottle while you invert it, and while its mouth is under water.

3. *Collecting by Use of both Methods at once.* — Put the water pan *B* (Fig. 11) in place of the bottle *e* (Fig. 8).

The Generator. — The materials from which the gas is to be set free may be put into (*a*) a side-neck flask (Fig. 8) or a side-neck tube (Fig. 10) ; or (*b*) a common flask, with stopper and bent glass delivery tube (Fig. 12). Or (*c*) in case no heat is to be applied, a bottle generator (Fig. 13) is very satisfactory. Select a bottle whose capacity is 300 to 500 cc., the mouth of which is 2.5 to 3 cm. inside diameter. Fit a sound cork or a rubber stopper with two tubes, — one a bent delivery tube (*b*), the other a " thistle tube " (*t*), which reaches nearly to the bottom of the bottle. Through this tube liquid can be poured at pleasure, while no gas can escape, because the lower end is closed by the liquid.

Fig. 12.

Fig. 13.

(*d*) The thistle tube may be used with any of the preceding forms of generator, if desired.

II. Study of Oxygen.

Oxygen may be obtained by heating mercuric oxide (Exp. 3) or potassium chlorate (Exp. 4). The chlorate is preferred ; and the chlorate will yield its oxygen more readily when mixed with manganese dioxide.

EXPERIMENT 11.

Object.— To liberate oxygen from potassium chlorate, and to discover its properties.

1. To Liberate and Collect the Gas.

Manipulation and Notes. — Take 6 g. of potassium chlorate and grind it to powder in a mortar. Add 3 g. of manganese dioxide. Mix the two powders. Put the mix-

ture into a side-neck tube. Cork the tube tightly, and fix
it in the clamp, as shown in Fig. 10 (p. 21).

Use four flasks and a bottle, with glass tubes (Fig. 8,
p. 20). Leave *a* empty. Cover the bottom of *b* with sand,
and add water, so that the end of the long tube shall be
just below the surface. Put a layer of water in the bottle
also. *Prove the joints to be air-tight.*

Heat the mixture in the generator, at first with a *low*
flame, and move the burner so as to heat the tube uniformly
(give reason). Gradually turn on a higher flame, and let it
play first against the upper part of the mixture *(give reason)*.
If at any time the gas is given off too fast (shown by the
bubbles in the water), remove the flame until the flow is
slackened. Note any change in the substances used. Observe how the gas drives the air from flask to flask, and out
at *e.*

When the bottle *e* is filled with O,[1] as you may learn
by means of a glowing splinter put just within its mouth,
you can put a water pan, previously made ready, in place
of the bottle *e*, covering this bottle with a glass plate, and
fill two or three bottles with gas by displacement of water
(Fig. 11).[2]

Disjoin the generator from *a* by taking the rubber tube
from *a*, and lower the flame to cool the tube slowly *(give
reason)*. Also take the rubber tube from the short tube of
the last flask.

[1] One or two letters are often written instead of the whole name
of an element. Thus O stands for oxygen, H stands for hydrogen,
and Cl stands for chlorine. In reading and speaking, however, use
the word: say "oxygen" rather than "O," etc. These abbreviations are called symbols. Every element has a symbol. See Table
of Elements, Appendix, A.

[2] Six grams of the chlorate is capable of yielding about 1.5 liters
of O. Some will be lost while collecting it *(give reason)*, so that the
total capacity of the apparatus used should not much exceed 1 liter.

2. To Discover the Properties of Oxygen.

Manipulation and Notes. — (*a*) What is its color? To discover its odor, test the gas in bottle *e* (*note*). Leave the bottle uncovered.

(*b*) Is it lighter or heavier than air? To answer this question, find, by a glowing taper, whether the gas still remains in the open bottle (*note*), and judge how the result bears on the question. Slip a glass plate under the mouth of a bottle which was filled by displacement of water; place the bottle on the table, mouth upward; uncover, and let it stand a full minute, then test with the glowing taper (*note*). If you have a second bottle filled, lift it from the water, mouth downward, and hold it in this position a full minute; test with the glowing splinter (*note*). Show how these results bear on the question.

(*c*) What is the effect of O on the burning of a candle? To find an answer, make a taper test (Fig. 14) as follows: Bend a wire as shown; then warm the lower end, and press it into the bottom of a piece of one of the smallest kind of wax candles. Light the taper, and lower the flame a little way into the flask *c* (*note*). Extinguish the flame, but leave a glow upon the wick; lower it into the gas (*note*). After the burning of the taper in the gas, pour a little limewater into the flask and shake it well (*note*). Compare results with those noted in Exp. 5, and explain.

Fig. 14.

(*d*) How will red-hot iron be affected by oxygen? Take a piece of small iron wire and bind about one third of a match to one end. Set fire to the match, and lower it into the mouth of the flask *b*, lowering still further as the action goes on (*note*). Be careful that the hot wire does not touch the glass (*give reason*).

III. Study of Hydrogen.

EXPERIMENT 12.

Object. — To liberate hydrogen from dilute sulphuric acid, and to discover its properties.

1. To Liberate Hydrogen from Dilute Sulphuric Acid.

Manipulation and Notes. — Put the materials into a side-neck flask, and collect the gas over water (Fig. 11, p. 22). A thistle tube is desirable. Refer to (*c*) and (*d*), p. 23.

To 60 cc. of water in a beaker add slowly, with stirring, 12 cc. of strong sulphuric acid. *Slide* fragments of zinc, 10 or 12 g. (it should not be dropped) into the flask. If a thistle tube is used, insert the stopper tightly. Pour the dilute acid through the thistle tube until the lower end is covered (*give reason*). More acid may be added as needed to keep up the action. If no thistle tube is used, pour the whole of the acid upon the zinc at once, and quickly close the flask. *Do not use the first bottleful collected (give reason)*, nor the second, if the bottles are smaller than the flask. After filling two or three small bottles with the gas, leaving them standing mouth downward in the water, proceed at once to discover the properties of the gas.

2. To Discover the Properties of Hydrogen.

Manipulation and Notes. — (*a*) What is its color and its odor ?

(*b*) Is this gas heavier, or lighter, than air ? To answer this question, fill a test tube by displacement of water. Close it with the thumb. Lift it from the water, keeping its mouth downward. Remove the thumb, and a little while afterward bring a lighted match to its mouth. Again proceed with another tube in the same way, *except* that you keep its mouth upward (*note*).

(c) To study the "explosibility" of hydrogen, fill a tube a third full of water, and displace this by H.[1] Consider what the tube now contains. Close it with the thumb. Lift it from the water. Hold it at arm's length, with its mouth downward. Remove the thumb, and at the same moment present the match flame to the mouth of the tube (*note*).

Fill the test tube *full* of water. Displace by H. Lift it and fire it as you did the one before. Compare the two results. Try to give a reason for the difference.

Can H burn without exploding? Try it with an apparatus shown in Fig. 15. Select a piece of glass tubing about the size of the stem of a 3-inch funnel, and cut from it a portion about 4 inches long. Heat the middle of this, constantly rolling it in the Bunsen flame until it softens, and then pull it lengthwise with both hands, and thus draw it out to the size of a knitting needle. Cut the small tube near the enlargement at one end. You now have a short tube which tapers down to a small opening. Fix this upon the stem of the funnel by a short rubber connection.

Select an evaporating dish large enough to let the funnel stand within it (a mortar may stand more firmly). Put enough dilute hydrochloric acid (half water) into the dish to well cover the edge of the funnel. Drop some pieces of zinc into the acid, and stand the funnel over it in the dish (Fig. 15). When the air has been all driven out (in about a minute, if the action

Fig. 15.

is brisk), you may touch a splinter flame to the gas jet, at arm's length.

The gas must come off steadily and freely. More zinc or more acid may be put under the funnel, if needed, *without letting any air enter* around its mouth. Note the first

[1] See note 1, p. 24.

effect, then what follows. Try to explain both, and point out the condition in which H is explosive.

(*d*) What is the product of burning H? Bring the mouth of a clean, dry, cold, wide-mouthed bottle down over the flame of H (Fig. 15) for a few moments (*note*). What do you infer the product to be? Is the evidence conclusive?

(*e*) To obtain dry H, take a "drying tube" (*a*, Fig. 16); put a little cotton wool into the bulb loosely; fill the tube nearly full of granulated calcium chloride,[1] and put a thin layer of cotton over it. Next close the large end with a cork pierced with a hole to receive the stem of the funnel. A small jet tube may be joined to the small end of this tube (*b*, Fig. 16).

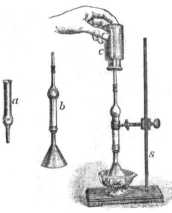

Fig. 16.

Put zinc into the dish. Place the funnel in the dish over it, and clamp the drying tube as shown. Pour dilute acid into the dish. Make the action steady and brisk.

(*f*) After waiting a minute or two, until sure that the air has been expelled, set fire to the H at the top of the jet, and then hold a wide-mouthed bottle, which is clean and dry, over the flame, as shown at *c*. What is now produced by the burning of H? Which is the more conclusive experiment, — (*d*) or (*f*)? Why?

[1] Calcium chloride absorbs moisture from air and gases very greedily.

III. ACIDS, BASES, AND SALTS.

EXPERIMENT 13.

Object. — To ascertain some characteristics of sulphuric acid.

Manipulation and Notes. — (*a*) What is its taste?[1] Try it in this way: Add a drop or two of the acid to a test tube nearly full of water. Mix them by stirring with a glass rod, and then present a small drop on the end of the rod to the tongue.

(*b*) How does it affect the color of litmus? To answer this, fill a bottle two thirds full of water, and add enough solution of blue litmus to color it distinctly. Next add dilute sulphuric acid (1 of acid to 10 of water) drop by drop.

(*c*) What is its action on a metal? For an answer, pour 5 cc. of strong sulphuric acid into 40 cc. of water in a bottle, drop into it some coarse iron filings or small nails, and cover the bottle with a square of heavy paper. In a few moments bring a lighted match to the mouth of the bottle, lifting the cover at the same moment. What chemical change may have taken place in this experiment? Set the bottle aside in order to examine its contents in Exp. 18.

EXPERIMENT 14.

Object. — To ascertain some characteristics of hydrochloric acid.

Manipulation and Notes. — Examine this acid with

---

[1] Most chemicals are poisonous or hurtful. *Tasting* should never be done by the student unless by direction found in the book or given by the instructor, and then only in the way directed.

reference to the same qualities exhibited by sulphuric acid in Exp. 13, and proceed by the same directions.

(*a*) What is its taste?

(*b*) How does it affect the color of litmus?

(*c*) To learn how it acts with a metal, use zinc, and treat it with acid diluted 1 to 3. Preserve the contents of this bottle for Exp. 18.

EXPERIMENT 15.

Object. — *To learn some characteristics of acetic acid.*

Manipulation and Notes. — Learn its taste and action on litmus by directions in Exp. 13 (*a*) and (*b*) (*note*). For its action on metal, put 10 cc. of the acid into a tube and drop upon it a short piece (about two inches) of magnesium ribbon (*note*). Preserve this result for Exp. 18.

Use iron instead of magnesium, and gently heat the acetic acid (*note*).

General. — Compare your results, and note three important respects in which sulphuric, hydrochloric, and acetic acids are alike. Other acids are like these three in these respects.

EXPERIMENT 16.

Object. — *To ascertain some characteristics of ammonium hydroxide.*

Manipulation and Notes. — (*a*) What is its taste? Proceed as directed in Exp. 13.

(*b*) How does it affect the color of litmus? Make ready two bottles, each half full of water colored with blue litmus. Stir the water in one bottle with a glass rod wet with an acid, and repeat, if necessary, until the color changes to red. Then add, drop by drop, ammonium hydroxide, first to the blue, and afterward to the reddened litmus.

EXPERIMENT 17.

Object. — *To compare some other hydroxide with ammonium hydroxide.*

Manipulation and Notes. — Solutions of sodium hydroxide, potassium hydroxide, and calcium hydroxide (lime-water) may be used. Proceed as you did with ammonium hydroxide, to answer questions (*a*) and (*b*).

General. — Compare the results, and note the common characteristics of these compounds. Other hydroxides are like these in these respects. Note also the characteristic differences between the hydroxides and the acids. Hydroxides are also called *bases.*

EXPERIMENT 18.

Object. — *To examine a product of the mutual action of a metal and an acid.*

Manipulation and Notes. — Use iron with sulphuric acid or examine the liquid saved from Exp. 13 (*c*) as follows: Pour off the clear liquid from the sediment or residue of iron into an evaporating dish, and evaporate "to crystallization;" i.e., until a solid appears when a drop is cooled on a glass rod or plate. Set the dish aside to cool spontaneously. Proceed at once to examine the liquids saved from Exps. 14 and 15 in the same way. It may be necessary to "evaporate to dryness" in some cases. Describe these products. Try also to explain the chemical changes which produced them.

General. — These compounds are *salts.* They have been produced by metals decomposing acids, driving hydrogen out, and substituting themselves in its place. Sulphuric acid with iron yielded the salt named iron sulphate, also called ferrous sulphate. Hydrochloric acid with zinc gave the salt named zinc chloride. Acetic acid yields salts called acetates, such as the magnesium acetate and the iron acetate of Exp. 15.

EXPERIMENT 19.

Object. — *To study the mutual action of acids and bases.*

Manipulation and Notes. — Use hydrochloric acid and sodium hydroxide. Put 5 cc. of hydrochloric acid into a bottle or beaker, and drop into it a small bit of litmus paper, which instantly becomes red. Next add a solution of sodium hydroxide, little by little, shaking or stirring the liquid well after each addition. Watch the color of the litmus paper; it will after a while show signs of turning blue. Then add the hydroxide carefully, a drop at a time, until after the last drop the paper remains blue. Then add a drop of *dilute* hydrochloric acid: the paper should neither be distinctly blue nor red, but purple. By this sign you know that the acid and base are neutralized by each other.

Next search for the product of the action. Put the liquid into a porcelain dish, and evaporate it carefully until *dry*. Let the residue cool. Note its color and its taste. What does it seem to be? Is it a salt, according to the definition of that term?

EXPERIMENT 20.

Object. — *To compare the products obtained by the action of the metal sodium, and of the sodium hydroxide, on hydrochloric acid.*

Manipulation and Notes. — (*a*) Measure 2 cc. of strong hydrochloric acid into a test tube which stands in the rack. Drop in upon it a piece of sodium as large as a very small pea, and instantly cover the mouth of the tube loosely with a piece of paper. After half a minute, test the gas with a match flame. When the sodium has disappeared, drop in another piece of about the same size, and afterward a third.

(*b*) To examine the product: Let it settle to the bottom of the tube, and then pour off the liquid so carefully that you leave the solid behind almost dry. In this way you get rid of most of the acid which was not decomposed. Then add water enough to dissolve the solid. Pour the solution into a small porcelain dish, and heat it over a *small flame* until the water is all driven off and the solid remains dry and white. The dish must now stand until cold, after which add a few drops of water. Taste the solution. Compare the product with that obtained in Exp. 19. Should you call this product a salt? Why?

General. — The action of the acid and base in Exp. 19 is typical. By their mutual action, when mixed in solution, an acid and a base neutralize each other, or, in other words, mutually decompose each other to form two new compounds, neither of which is an acid or a base. One of them is a *salt :* the other is water. The foregoing experiments show that salts may be produced in two ways (*explain*).

3

IV. DEFINITE PROPORTIONS.

EXPERIMENT 21.

Object. — To ascertain whether, when hydrochloric acid and sodium hydroxide neutralize each other, there is any particular relation between the quantities required.

Manipulation and Notes. — Mix 2 cc. of hydrochloric acid with 100 cc. of water. Mix 15 cc. of sodium-hydroxide solution with 100 cc. of water. Prepare two burettes. Rinse one with water, and then with 2 or 3 cc. of the dilute hydrochloric acid, and support it in a clamp (*h*, Fig. 17). Rinse the other with water, and afterward with 2 or 3 cc. of the dilute sodium hydroxide, and support it in a clamp, *s.* See that the tips of both are closed by their pinchcocks.

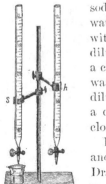

Fig. 17.

Fill the burette *h* with the dilute acid, and the burette *s* with the dilute hydroxide. Draw off from each by pressing the pinchcock until the *bottom* of the meniscus (the curved upper surface of the liquid) is exactly level with the zero mark on the burette. (Be careful to place your eye on a level with the mark, so that your sight shall not slant upward or downward.)

Run out exactly 10 cc. of the acid into a small beaker, and add a drop of litmus solution. Then add from the burette *s* the hydroxide little by little, keeping it mixed by shaking the beaker, and toward the last carefully, drop by drop, until the change of color to purplish blue shows that the acid is neutralized. Note the number of cubic centimeters used.

Repeat, using 15 cc. of the acid; and again, using 20 cc. of the acid. Then find in each case the *ratio* of the quantities of acid and base, extending the division to one decimal place.

Record your results in tabular form, as follows: —

Acid used.	Hydroxide required.	cc. of Hydroxide for 1 cc. Acid.
10 cc.	.... cc.	....
15 cc.	.... cc.	....
20 cc.	.... cc.	....

Are the quantities of base for 1 cc. of acid very different?

Is the difference so small that it may be due to the necessary lack of exactness (*give reason*) in your experiment?

Would you conclude that a given quantity of one of these liquids would in every case require a definite quantity of the other, or not?

Does each cubic centimeter of this dilute acid contain the same mass of acid as every other? Does the chemical action take place between definite masses, or without regard to the proportions?

EXPERIMENT 22.

Object. — *To ascertain whether, when hydrochloric acid and sodium carbonate react, there is any definite relation between the mass of the carbonate used and the mass of sodium chloride produced.*

Manipulation and Notes. — (*a*) Weigh a *clean* and dry porcelain dish. Add 5 g. of crystallized sodium carbonate, selecting small crystals which have no white spots (*give reason*). Pour in dilute hydrochloric acid little by little, until the carbonate is dissolved, taking care that no loss occurs by effervescence.

Place the dish over a small flame, and evaporate slowly to dryness, without loss, which toward the end of the operation requires watchful care. Do not press the heat after the salt is dry, else loss will occur by decrepitation (*give reason*). When cold, see that the outside of the dish is clean and dry, and then weigh it with its contents.

> Weight of dish and sodium chloride = ... g.
> Weight of dish alone   .... g.
> Weight of the sodium chloride   = ... g.

Hence 5 g. of sodium carbonate yield .... g. of sodium chloride.

(*b*) Repeat the foregoing operations with 10 g. of sodium carbonate.

Compare the results of (*a*) and (*b*),[1] and decide whether equal masses of sodium carbonate will yield the same mass of sodium chloride.

---

[1] It is well to give different quantities of sodium carbonate to different members of a class, and thus secure more data for discussion.

V. WATER.

EXPERIMENT 23.

Object. — To ascertain whether water is usually pure.

Manipulation and Notes. — (*a*) Does it hold any solid impurity? Evaporate to dryness 100 cc. of ordinary spring or hydrant water in a porcelain dish (*note*).

(*b*) Does it hold any gaseous impurity? Fill a flask, 1,000 cc. capacity (a smaller one will serve), with freshly drawn spring or hydrant water. Invert it, and leave it standing, mouth down, in a water pan for several hours, in a warm place (*note*).

(*c*) Evaporate some recently caught rain water, and compare its purity with that of water used in operation (*a*).

What are the constituents of pure water? (See Exp. 12.)

EXPERIMENT 24.

Object. — To discover the effect of contact of water with some solid substances.

Manipulation and Notes. — (*a*) Fill a bottle three fourths full of clear water. Cover it with a piece of muslin loosely, and bind the cover in place by a string around the neck (Fig. 18). Mix half a teaspoonful of powdered cochineal with a larger quantity of sand or soil. Place the mixture on the cover, and then pour some clear water slowly upon it. What is the result?

The liquid which you obtain is called a solution of cochineal. What would you obtain by evaporating it? Try it.

(b) Repeat the experiment, but in place of the cochineal use some powdered copper sulphate (note).

Fig. 18.

Name the liquid you obtain. Prove, by evaporation, that it contains copper sulphate.

Can you now explain the presence of solid impurities in spring water?

Is the dissolving of copper sulphate a chemical change?

EXPERIMENT 25.

Object. — *To ascertain whether the quantity of a solid soluble in a given volume of water is limited.*

Manipulation and Notes. — Measure 10 cc. of water into a test tube. Reduce the given solid to fine powder. Introduce a small portion. Close the tube with the thumb, and shake vigorously. If this portion is completely dissolved, add a second, and proceed as before; then perhaps a third. In any case, continue to add small portions until your object is accomplished. Use (a) copper sulphate, (b) sodium chloride, (c) barium sulphate.

Place these tubes with their contents aside, to be used in the next experiment.

If the first small portion does not disappear, so that you cannot decide whether any at all has been dissolved, you should decant the clear water from the solid, or filter it, and then evaporate it to dryness.

Write your conclusion. Point out the difference observed in the three substances.

EXPERIMENT 26.

Object. — *To ascertain the effect of heat on the solvent power of water.*

Manipulation and Notes. — Warm the tube containing the excess of solid which could not dissolve in cold water, and observe whether the solid disappears. Continue the heat, if need be, until the water boils. If in any case the solid disappears, add another small portion and continue the heat. Repeat until the liquid is *saturated ;* i.e., contains all it can hold of the solid in solution.

Use tubes (*a*), (*b*), and (*c*) of the preceding experiment. Write your conclusion with respect to each substance. Let the tubes stand until cold (*note ; explain*).

EXPERIMENT 27.

Object. — *To ascertain the solubility of a solid.*

Explanation. — The solubility of a solid is described in two ways, — either by stating *the mass* (usually called the weight) which can be dissolved in 100 cc. of the solvent, or by stating the volume of the saturated liquid which holds a unit of mass (1 g. of the solid) in solution.

Manipulation and Notes. — (*a*) For the solubility of barium chloride, place 20 cc. of water in a large test tube or small beaker. Add a portion of finely powdered chloride, and gradually heat to boiling. If this portion completely dissolves, add another. Repeat until the hot liquid is saturated. Cool the solution (*note*). When quite cold, filter it. Measure 15 cc. of the clear solution into a *weighed*, clean porcelain dish, and evaporate to dryness. *Let no loss occur.*

Cover the dish, and let it cool. When quite cold, see that the outside of the dish is clean, and weigh[1] it.

$$\text{Mass of dish and residue} = \text{............ g.}$$
$$\text{Mass of dish} \qquad\qquad = \text{............ g.}$$
$$\text{Mass of the residue alone} = \text{............ g. .... A}$$

$15 \div A = \text{.... } B = $ No. cc. of solution holding 1 g. of barium chloride.

The solubility of barium chloride in cold water is 1 g. to B cc.

[1] The balance gives the *masses* of bodies, but the masses are proportional to the *weights* in any one locality.

(*b*)[1] Find the solubility of sodium chloride in cold water.

(*c*) Find the solubility of copper sulphate in cold water.

EXPERIMENT 28.

Object. — *To learn whether water boils at any particular temperature.*

Manipulation and Notes. — Put water into an open flask, and support it by a clamp.   Heat it gradually.   Put the bulb of a thermometer into the water, and watch its indications.   Continue this until the water boils freely, and for some time afterward (*note*).   Raise the bulb into the vapor above the water (*note, and draw conclusions*).

EXPERIMENT 29.

Object. — *To determine the boiling point of water.*

Manipulation and Notes. — Place sufficient water in a side-neck flask to fill it about one fourth full, and close it with a cork through which extends the stem of a thermometer, as shown in Fig. 19, the bulb a little below the opening into the side neck.   To the side neck join a long glass tube by a rubber connection.   Put the end of the glass tube down into a test tube which rests

Fig. 19.

in the water pan nearly filled with *cold* water, and finally heat the flask with a Bunsen lamp.

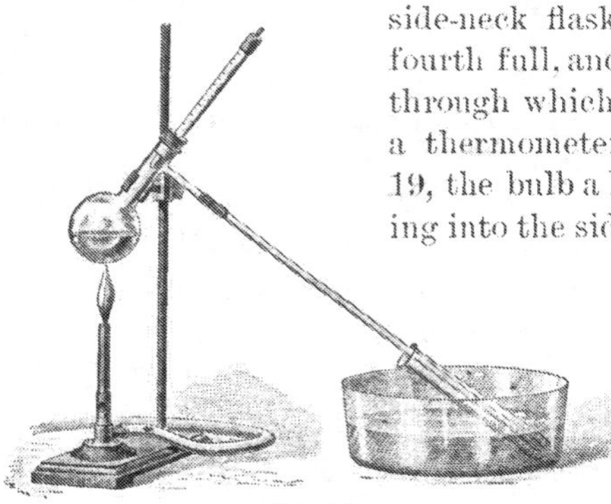

[1] A class may very well be divided into sections, to each of which a single substance is assigned.   The results of all may be discussed together.

Note *every* effect you can see while the water is being heated, but especially the effect on its temperature before and during the ebullition. If the temperature becomes constant while the water boils, read and note it as the boiling point.

Examine the substance in the test tube. What is it, and how came it there? Decide, by evaporating it, whether it is purer than the water in the flask.

General. — In like manner the boiling points of other liquids may be found. The object of the delivery tube, test tube, and water pan is to collect the substance instead of letting it pass into the air. They may be dispensed with if there is no objection to letting the vapor escape. When the vapor is collected and condensed, the process is called *distillation.* This is the most important method of purifying water and other liquids.

EXPERIMENT 30.

Object. — *To compare the boiling points of water and alcohol.*

Repeat Exp. 29 with alcohol instead of water.

EXPERIMENT 31.

Object. — *To find the density of water and of alcohol.*

Explanation. — The density of a substance is described by stating the mass of the substance contained in 1 cc. or in a unit volume.

$$\text{Density} = \frac{\text{Mass in grams}}{\text{Volume in cubic centimeters}}$$

Manipulation and Notes. — (*a*) Weigh a clean, dry beaker; add 20 cc. of cold water; take its temperature; weigh the beaker and water, and make the necessary calculation. Finally state your result as follows: —

RESULT: The density of water at .....° C. is ..... g. per cc.

(*b*) Repeat the operations, using alcohol at the temperature of the room. State the result as follows : —

RESULT: The density of alcohol at .....° C. is ..... g. per cc.

Divide the density of alcohol by that of water. The *quotient* is the *relative* density of alcohol. State your result as follows : —

RESULT: The relative density of alcohol at .....° C. is.....

General. — In like manner, the densities and the relative densities of other liquids may be found.

EXPERIMENT 32.

Object. — *To compare the action of water with that of hydrochloric acid on sodium carbonate.*

Manipulation and Notes. — Place 1 g. of sodium carbonate in a small porcelain dish, add about 5 cc. of water, and stir the mixture until the solid disappears (*note*). To learn whether a chemical change has occurred, evaporate the solution to dryness, and see whether the carbonate is restored unchanged (*note*).

Add *dilute* hydrochloric acid to 1 g. of sodium carbonate until the solid is dissolved (*note*). Evaporate the solution slowly, compare the dry product with the original carbonate (*note*), and judge whether a chemical change occurred.

General. — These results should show that solutions sometimes involve only physical changes, and sometimes chemical changes. Water solutions are usually physical solutions; acid solutions are usually chemical. With dilute acid the action is both physical and chemical. In this experiment, for example, the carbonate was chemically changed into the chloride, and then the water which was present dissolved the chloride without change.

VI. HYDROCHLORIC–ACID AND OTHER CHLORIDES.

EXPERIMENT 33.

Object. — *To obtain hydrochloric acid, and study its properties.*

Manipulation and Notes. — (*a*) Hydrochloric acid may be prepared by the mutual action of sodium chloride and sulphuric acid. To 12 cc. of water in a beaker add slowly, and with constant stirring, 33 cc. of strong sulphuric acid. While this acid is cooling, set up the apparatus, consisting of a side-neck flask, three conical flasks, and a bottle. The connections would better be all glass (Fig. 8, p. 20). The flasks should be dry. Connect flasks *a* and *b* with long tubes toward the generator. Join *c* with short tube toward generator, and to its long tube join a delivery tube reaching into the bottle. Put 50 cc. of water into the bottle, and let the tube dip into it. All joints should be proved to be tight. When the connections are all made, put into the generator about 35 g. of sodium chloride. Pour upon it rapidly the 45 cc. of the cold diluted acid, and quickly insert the stopper of the flask. Close the holes of a Bunsen burner; turn the flame down to a height less than an inch; place it below the generator, with the flame not touching the glass. If the gas is given off too rapidly, remove the heat until it slackens. Describe all the changes. Note especially what takes place in the water, and explain it.

(*b*) Remove the stopper from flask *b*, and invert the flask with its mouth in a vessel of water (*note*).

What property of the gas does this result reveal?

(c) What is its behavior toward flame? Remove the stopper from c, and insert a splinter flame (*note*). Then invert the flask in water (*give reason*).

(d) How does its solution behave toward litmus? Place blue-litmus solution in a test tube, and add a little of the gas solution from the bottle (*note*).

(e) How does it behave toward solution of silver nitrate? To a very dilute solution of silver nitrate in a test tube add a few drops of the gas solution (*note*).[1]

End the Experiment. — If the generator is cold, close its side neck. Invert it with its mouth under water in a pan. When the gas has been all absorbed, the flasks and generator may be emptied and cleansed.

EXPERIMENT 34.

Object. — *To liberate chlorine from hydrochloric acid.*

Manipulation and Notes. — Put 1 or 2 g. of manganese dioxide in a test tube by sliding it to the bottom along a little paper trough (in this way you keep the oxide from soiling the tube). Pour upon the oxide 1 cc. of strong hydrochloric acid. Close the tube loosely with the finger. Wait until the acid has moistened the oxide completely, and then warm it by holding it above the tip of a very low flame. Just as soon as the tube seems almost full of the product, remove the heat. (Caution: do not breathe this gas! Do not drive it off into the air.) Describe the gas.

Cautiously open the tube and insert a narrow strip of blue litmus paper (*note*).

End the Experiment. — Invert the tube and uncover its mouth under water. Leave it thus so long as gas can be seen in it. What property of the gas does this result reveal?

[1] The liquid hydrochloric acid of the laboratory is a strong solution of hydrochloric-acid gas in water.

EXPERIMENT 35.

Object. — *To study the mutual action of hydrochloric acid and iron.*

Manipulation and Notes. — Into 5 cc. of strong hydrochloric acid put several small bits of iron, such as small tacks. Test the gas (*note*). Let the tube stand until the action is over. Describe the solution. Obtain the solid from solution by filtering and evaporation. Describe this *ferrous chloride.*

General. — This experiment is typical. Several other metals may be converted into their chlorides in the same way.

EXPERIMENT 36.

Object. — *To study the effect of nitric acid upon the action of hydrochloric acid and iron.*

Manipulation and Notes. — (*a*) Dissolve the ferrous chloride obtained in Exp. 35 in a little water. Add a few drops of strong nitric acid, and heat to boiling (*note*). Evaporate, and compare residue with the ferrous chloride used.

(*b*) Put 2 cc. of strong hydrochloric acid into a test tube, and add about one fourth as much strong nitric acid (*note*). Into this drop two or three small tacks (*note*).

When the action is over, evaporate, and decide whether the residue is ferrous chloride or the substance found in (*a*), or something else.

General. — This experiment is typical. Nitric acid changes the lower compounds of many substances into the higher as it changed the ferrous chloride into ferric chloride in (*a*). On this account it is called an *oxidizing agent.* A mixture of strong hydrochloric acid and strong nitric acid is known as *aqua regia.* It contains free chlorine, and chlorine in unstable combination, by which the highest chloride of a metal is formed at once, as in (*b*).

VII. THE CHLORINE GROUP.

EXPERIMENT 37.

Object. — *To liberate chlorine, iodine, and bromine from their compounds of sodium or potassium.*

Manipulation and Notes. — (*a*) *Chlorine.* Pour 1 cc. of strong sulphuric acid into 1 cc. of water in a test tube. Mix, and set aside to cool. Mix ½ g. of dry sodium chloride with ½ g. of manganese dioxide. When the acid is cold, introduce the mixture of salt and oxide without soiling the walls of the tube. Cover the tube with the finger, hold it nearly horizontal, and warm the mixture *very gently.* Withdraw the heat as soon as the action is well started, that the gas shall not be driven into the air. *Do not breathe the gas* nor air containing much of it (*note*). Lower a splinter flame just into the upper layer of the gas (*note*). Lower a narrow strip of litmus paper into the gas (*note*). Finally invert the tube in a pan of water to keep the gas out of the atmosphere. Write and explain the reaction which occurred.

(*b*) *Bromine.* Proceed exactly as in (*a*), using ½ g. of sodium or potassium bromide mixed with 1 g. of manganese dioxide, and 1 cc. of acid prepared by adding 1 cc. of strong sulphuric acid to 5 cc. of water. *Do not breathe the vapors!* Note color and odor. Observe the cold walls of the tube (*note*). Introduce a splinter flame just inside the mouth of the tube (*note*). Introduce a strip of moist litmus paper (*note*). Invert in water. Write and explain the reaction by which bromine was set free.

(c) *Iodine.* Proceed exactly as in (*a*), using acid of the same strength with a mixture of **1** g. of sodium or potassium iodide with **2** g. of manganese dioxide. Do not breathe the vapors (*note*). Test with flame (*note*) and with litmus paper (*note*). Observe the upper cold walls of the tube (*note*). Invert in water. Note whether the chlorine, the bromine, and the iodine are absorbed by the water, and judge their solubilities. Write and explain the reaction by which iodine was set free.

(d) Put a few crystals of iodine into a dry tube, and add a very little alcohol. Judge the solubility of iodine in alcohol (*note*). The strong solution is called *tincture of iodine.*

General. — In the foregoing study you can detect the very great chemical resemblance of the three elements (*explain*). You also find some marked differences (*explain*). Their chemical resemblance is shown in all their reactions, and in the composition of all their compounds.

EXPERIMENT 38.

Object. — *To compare the chemical actions of chlorides, bromides, and iodides.*

Manipulation and Notes. — 1. *With Silver Nitrate.* Arrange three test tubes with 2 cc. of pure water in each. Add to one, 5 drops of strong solution of any chloride (sodium chloride); to a second, 5 drops of a strong solution of any bromide (potassium); and to a third, 5 cc. of any iodide (potassium). Treat the mixtures in succession as follows: —

(a) Add silver nitrate drop by drop, shaking the tube vigorously after each addition, until a drop fails to make a precipitate. Describe the precipitates. Note the effect of shaking them. Look carefully for some difference in their colors.

(b) Then expose the tubes to sunlight, or for some time to diffuse light, and note the changes which occur in the colors.

Which are most marked, — the resemblances, or the differences, seen in these reactions ? Note the differences with care.

(c) Next test the solubility of these precipitates in ammonium hydrate. To do this, make a little fresh precipitate, and keep it from light as much as possible. When the precipitate has settled, decant the liquid carefully, so as to leave the precipitate in the tube. Then pour upon it ammonium hydrate gradually, with shaking, until you can decide whether the precipitate dissolves.

Compare the solubilities with care (note).

2. *With Starch.* Make a very thin starch water by boiling a minute piece of starch in considerable water, and cooling the liquid. Dissolve a chloride, a bromide, and an iodide, each in water, but with this difference : make the bromide very concentrated, and the iodide very dilute.

To a part of each solution add a few drops of nitric acid, with this difference : for the iodide use the acid diluted one to one.   Add a little of the starch water. There should be a difference in color produced : note it carefully.

To another part of each solution add a little of the cold starch water, without the nitric acid. By this means you can decide whether nitric acid is necessary to bring out the colors observed before.

Add the starch water to hot solutions instead of cold ones, and let them become cold. By this means you will learn the effect of heat.

Compare the chloride, bromide, and iodide in these reactions with great care. Note differences.

General. — In this study you have found more proof of the chemical resemblance of chlorine, bromine, and iodine. You have also seen the *differences* by which you would be able to distinguish chlorides, bromides, and iodides from one another.

For practice, take a few substances from the teacher, or a friend who knows what they are, and see if you can decide whether each is a chloride, a bromide, or an iodide.

4

VIII. SULPHUR AND SOME OF ITS COMPOUNDS.

I. Sulphur and the Sulphides.

EXPERIMENT 39.

Object. — *To ascertain the effect of heat on sulphur.*

Manipulation and Notes. — Reduce a piece of brimstone to small fragments, and half fill a test tube with it. Hold the tube in the hot air above the lamp flame, and thus keep it from contact with too strong a heat, but lower it until you find the heat just intense enough to melt the sulphur. Can you melt it without changing the color of the liquid (*note*) ?

Place the tube with the limpid liquid sulphur where it will not be shaken, and watch the liquid while it slowly cools (*note*).

Now carefully re-melt the sulphur, and then make the liquid a little hotter, — only a little (*note*).

Continue to heat the liquid gradually, and incline the tube from time to time, until it is nearly horizontal (*note*).

Then heat it still more, and test from time to time its power to flow.

Continue to apply heat to find out whether the sulphur can be boiled, and what is the color of the vapor (*note*).

Pour the somewhat viscid, dark liquid in a small stream into a vessel of cold water, and examine the sulphur after this sudden cooling (*note*).

EXPERIMENT 40.

Object. — *To convert copper into copper sulphide.*

Manipulation and Notes. — Prepare a small coil of fine copper wire by winding the wire around a glass tube. Heat a small piece of sulphur to boiling in a tube. Insert the coil, and continue the heat for a minute. Describe the change which the copper has undergone.

The experiment may be made by mixing 4 g. of flowers of sulphur with 8 g. of fine copper filings, and heating this mixture in a test tube (*note*).

General. — This experiment is typical. Similarly many other metals may be converted into their sulphides by the direct action of sulphur.

EXPERIMENT 41.

Object. — *To obtain hydrogen sulphide from hydrochloric acid and ferrous sulphide.*

Manipulation and Notes. — Put a piece of ferrous sulphide not larger than a grain of wheat into a test tube, and pour upon it 1 cc. of dilute hydrochloric acid (half water) (*note*).

Notice *with care* the odor in the tube (*note*).

Test the gas with flame (*note*).

Notice the color of the liquid when the action is over.

Write and explain the reaction.

General. — This experiment typifies the action of strong acids on sulphides generally. It also teaches, that, in the preparation and use of hydrogen sulphide, there should be the utmost care to prevent its escape into the room (*give reason*).

Given a metallic compound, how would you proceed to determine whether it is a sulphide?

EXPERIMENT 42.

Object. — *To prepare hydrogen sulphide, and to learn something of its character.*

Manipulation and Notes. — Set up the usual gas apparatus, consisting of a side-neck flask, with three collecting flasks, *a, b, c,* and bottle (Fig. 8, p. 20). Put water enough in *a* to cover the end of the long tube when inserted. Put about the same quantity in *b,* and add 1 cc. of solution of copper chloride. Put water and a little zinc-acetate solution in *c,* and into the bottle put dilute ammonium hydroxide (half water). Connect with long tubes toward generator. *Prove the joints to be air-tight (give reason).*

Finally slide about 10 g. of ferrous sulphide into the flask. Add 30 cc. of hydrochloric acid (half water). Quickly close the flask air-tight. Pay careful attention to what occurs in each flask in succession (*note*).

Let the action go on until effervescence ceases. Then disconnect *c* and the bottle, also *a* and the generator. Open the side-neck flask. Quickly cover its mouth with the hand, and invert it in water in the water pan (*give reason*).

Proceed with the study as follows: Take flask *a* out of the series without removing the stopper; transfer a little of its water to separate tubes, and proceed to ascertain (*a*) the odor of the water, (*b*) the effect of adding it to a dilute solution of copper chloride, (*c*) the effect of adding it to a dilute solution of zinc acetate.

Compare these actions of the water with the actions of the gas itself.

End the Experiment. — Invert each flask in water; remove the stopper, and leave it standing for some hours.

General. — The effects of H_2S [1] on copper chloride and

[1] The symbols of the elements in a compound are often written instead of the name of the compound. Thus, H_2S stands for hydro-

zinc acetate are typical. Similarly, the gas or its solution will convert the compounds of several other metals into sulphides.

II. Sulphuric Acid and Sulphates.

EXPERIMENT 43.

Object. — To study the mutual action of strong sulphuric acid and water.

Manipulation and Notes. — Into a wide-mouthed bottle pour 40 cc. of cold water. Then pour into it gradually, while you stir it, 40 cc. of strong sulphuric acid. Feel the sides of the bottle (*note*). Insert a test tube holding a little alcohol (*note*).

General. — The evolution of heat is evidence of chemical action.

Sulphuric acid combines readily with the constituents of water whenever the two liquids are brought together.

EXPERIMENT 44.

Object. — To study the action of sulphuric acid on wood.

Manipulation and Notes. — Put 2 or 3 cc. of strong acid into a test tube, and place in it the end of a clean pine stick. After a few minutes rinse the stick with water (*note*). The constituents of wood are chiefly carbon, hydrogen, and oxygen. In the light of Exp. 43, how would you explain the change in the wood? Use paper instead of wood (*note*).

General. — These results are typical. All organic substances are affected in a similar way by this acid.

gen sulphide, because hydrogen (H) and sulphur (S) are its constituents. The small figure 2 shows that there are two combining weights of H to one of S. Such abbreviations are called formulas. See list of chemicals, Appendix, C, 2.

EXPERIMENT 45.

Object. — *To study the action of sulphuric acid on metals.*

Manipulation and Notes. — Put a small piece of the given metal into a test tube. Cover it with dilute acid. Close the tube loosely with the finger. If a gas is set free, test it; but if no action begins soon, apply a gentle heat (*note*). If still there is no action, pour off the dilute, and add a little concentrated acid, and proceed as before (*note*).

When the action is ended, filter, evaporate the liquid, and describe the substance obtained.

Use magnesium in the form of ribbon or wire. Repeat or recall the results of Exps. 7 and 13 (*c*). *Do not breathe the gases!*

General. — The solids obtained by action of sulphuric acid on the metals are *sulphates.* These experiments are typical.

III. Sulphur Dioxide and Sulphites.

EXPERIMENT 46.

Object. — *To prepare and examine the gas liberated by action of sulphuric acid and copper.*

Manipulation and Notes. — (*a*) Set up a gas apparatus, consisting of side-neck flask, three collecting flasks, *a*, *b*, *c*, a water pan, and bottle. The connections would better be all glass. Put about 15 g. of copper clippings into the generator; leave *a* empty; put about 30 cc. of water into *b*, and about 30 cc. of water containing about 2 g. of potassium hydroxide into *c*. Then connect with long tubes toward the generator, their lower ends well covered with water in the flasks.

Prove the joints to be air-tight. Pour about 25 cc. of strong sulphuric acid upon the copper, and close the generator.

Apply a *gentle* heat until the action is well started, but no longer. Warm again if the action slackens, and keep a slow and steady bubbling of gas through the water in *b*. When the odor of the gas can be detected at *c*, add a delivery tube, and collect the overflow of gas by displacement of water.

Describe and explain whatever occurs in every part of the apparatus, and draw all possible inferences about the properties of the gas.

When the liquid in *c* is saturated (*how known*), disconnect the generator, and at once join the side neck to the short tube of an empty flask, and connect the long tube with a delivery tube inserted in a strong solution of sodium hydroxide (*give reason*). Disconnect all the flasks. Then proceed to examine the gas.

(*b*) Determine its effect on fire by a splinter flame in the mouth of *a*. The stopper should be at once replaced.

(*c*) Determine the behavior of its solution toward litmus by adding to litmus solution in a tube a small portion from *b* without removing the stopper. Is it acid, or basic, or neutral?

(*d*) Determine its effect on a solution of logwood by adding a portion from *b* to a tube containing the colored liquid previously made by boiling a few chips of logwood in water.

Try its action on other colors. Suspend a small flower or a few petals in *a*, or in a bottle full of gas.

(*e*) Consider what chemical action may have occurred in the potassium hydroxide. Evaporate the saturated solution of the gas in flask *c*. In the mean time invert the collecting flasks with open mouths under water, and leave standing (*give reason*). Is the residue obtained by evaporation the potassium hydroxide which was put into *c*? Decide by treating it with a little hydrochloric acid.

General. — The foregoing experiments have revealed the most prominent characteristics of sulphur dioxide (*name* *them*); its action on certain coloring matters, which renders it useful as a bleaching agent in the arts; and its chemical relations to water and bases (*explain*). The salts formed by the action of its solution on hydroxides are *sulphites*.

(*f*) Judging from Exp. 18 and the definition of the term *salt*, what salt should have been produced by the sulphuric acid and copper in the foregoing work? Can you see any indications of this salt in the side-neck flask? To test this supposition, proceed to examine the residue in the flask, as follows: —

Decant the liquid from the flask, leaving all solid residue behind. Put about 50 cc. of water into the flask, shake it well, and let it stand awhile (*note*). Finally filter; evaporate the filtrate to crystallization; let stand for crystals to form. Decant the liquid, dry the crystals by contact with filter paper, and decide whether they are the salt you predicted.

IV. Comparison of Sulphides, Sulphites, and Sulphates.

EXPERIMENT 47.

Object. — *To study the action of dilute acids on sulphides, sulphites, and sulphates.*

Manipulation and Notes. — (*a*) Put a little of the powder of some specimen of each of these compounds into a separate tube, moisten it with water, and add a little dilute hydrochloric acid. Watch for effervescence, and any other evidence of chemical action. Notice the odor of any gas which may be set free. If no action begins soon, heat may be used (*note*).

(*b*) Use dilute sulphuric acid, making the experiments in the same way (*note*).

Point out the *difference* in the behavior of these three classes of compounds toward the dilute acids used.

EXPERIMENT 48.

Object. — *To study the action of barium chloride on sulphites and sulphates.*

Manipulation and Notes. — (*a*) Add drops of barium chloride to a solution of a sulphite and to a solution of a sulphate. Then compare the precipitates which appear.

(*b*) Learn, by experiment, whether these two precipitates are alike soluble in hydrochloric acid.

(*c*) See whether both these precipitates will appear if you add the hydrochloric acid to the solutions before you add the barium chloride.

Point out the resemblance in the behavior of these two classes of compounds toward barium chloride. State clearly the condition in which their behavior toward barium chloride differs.

From the foregoing experiments one may make a plan by which to decide whether a given substance is a sulphide, or a sulphite, or a sulphate. Try to do this.

For practice, take from the teacher, or a friend who knows what they are, a few substances, and see if you can decide whether each is a sulphide, or a sulphite, or a sulphate.

IX. NITROGEN.

EXPERIMENT 49.

Object. — *To obtain nitrogen by burning the oxygen out of air with sulphur.*

Manipulation and Notes. — Cut a slice half an inch thick from a cork which is much smaller than the mouth of

a bottle. Shape the top of the cork into a shallow cup, and cover it with a paste of moistened plaster of Paris. Let the plaster become dry, then put sulphur in this cup, place it on the shallow water in a water pan, set fire to the sulphur, and put the bottle bottom upward over it,

Fig. 20.

as shown in Fig. 20. Describe the flame of the sulphur, the action of the water when the burning is over, the change in the gas after long time standing. The gas obtained at last is nitrogen.

EXPERIMENT 50.

Object. — *To obtain nitrogen by burning the oxygen out of air with phosphorus.*

Manipulation and Notes. — Follow the directions given above for burning sulphur, but use a piece of phosphorus not larger than a good-sized kernel of wheat, with a smaller bottle holding about 200 cc., and observe the following precautions.

Precautions. — The handling of phosphorus is dangerous unless it is done with great care. Phosphorus takes fire easily, and burns the flesh cruelly. Therefore cut it under water, lift the piece with the knife blade, dry it by gentle contact with filter paper, and put it into a *dry* cup. Never handle phosphorus without using the greatest care. *Red phosphorus* may be used with less danger than the common yellow variety.

Set fire to the phosphorus by touching it with a warm wire (*note*).

Let the bottle stand until its contents become colorless (*explain*).

EXPERIMENT 51.

Object. — To discover the properties of nitrogen.

Manipulation and Notes. — (*a*) What is the color of this gas?

(*b*) What is its action with a burning splinter? Slip a square of glass or of cardboard under the mouth of a bottle containing the gas, lift it out of the water, turn it mouth upward, stand it on the table, and leave it covered. At once ignite a splinter of wood, uncover the bottle, and insert the flame just inside its mouth. Leave the bottle uncovered. Treat the other bottle of gas in the same way. Leave this bottle also uncovered.

(*c*) Is it heavier, or lighter, than air? The bottles having now stood some minutes uncovered, again insert a flame into the bottle first left uncovered, and afterward into the other.

Tests. — How would you decide whether a given colorless gas is nitrogen, or hydrogen, or oxygen?

X. ANALYSIS OF AIR.

Object. — *To determine approximately the relative proportion of oxygen to other constituents of air.*

Manipulation and Notes. — Support a glass tube 15
to 30 cm. long and about 2 cm. wide, and closed at one end,
so that it will stand with its open end under water in a
water pan. Cut from small copper wire a piece about two
thirds the length of the tube. Cut from a stick of phosphorus a piece about as large as a bean of medium size.
Press the end of the wire (under water) into this. Thrust
the phosphorus end of the wire up into the glass tube, and
bring the mouth of the tube down again at once into the
water. Notice whether any action sets in. Let the action
go on until it ends: it will require several hours, perhaps
until next day.

Then note any changes. Mark the level of the water in
the tube by a rubber band or a thread.

Cover the mouth of the tube closely with the thumb.
Lift it and turn its mouth upward, letting no air enter,
and test the gas within by a lighted splinter. What is the
result? Decide what the phosphorus has taken out, and
what is left.

Find the volume of the gas that was left by measuring
the water required to fill the tube up to the rubber band.
Find the volume of the air which was used by measuring
the water required to fill the tube. Find the volume of

the gas absorbed by taking the difference. Note results thus : —

Volume of air used = ... cc.
Volume of oxygen absorbed = ... cc.
Volume of nitrogen and other gases = ... cc.

What fractional part of the air is oxygen?
What fractional part of the air is nitrogen and other gases?
How many cubic centimeters of oxygen in 100 cc. of air?

EXPERIMENT 53.

Object. — *To find out how many cubic centimeters of nitrogen, and how many of oxygen and carbon dioxide, there are in 100 cc. of air.*

Plan. — To do this, we will imprison a vesselful of air, and then run into it a liquid which will absorb both the oxygen and the carbon dioxide completely, and leave the nitrogen. We can then measure the nitrogen which is left, and we can find out how much there was of the other two by measuring the liquid which has gone into the tube to take their place.

The Apparatus. — Take a test tube (*t*, Fig. 21) to hold the air. A 6-inch tube, $\frac{5}{8}$ of an inch in diameter, will do; an 8-inch tube of the same diameter is better. The rubber stopper *c* is so large, that its small end will enter the tube only about a half inch. It has two holes. To close one, use a solid rod of glass, *s ;* into the other put a glass tube reaching just a very little below the cork, as shown. A piece of thin rubber tubing, *h*, is cut about 6 inches long. There is a pinchcock, *p*, by which its walls may be pinched so as to close it completely. *F* is a small glass funnel.

Fig. 21.

Stretch the lower end of *h* over the tube in the cork *c*,

and fix its upper end over the stem of *F.* Then place the funnel in the clamp of the support, as shown in Fig. 22, and remove the rod *s.*

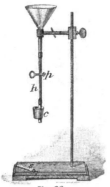

Fig. 22.

The Liquid. — To absorb the oxygen and carbon dioxide gases, use a mixture of pyrogallic acid and potassium hydroxide.

Take a small teaspoonful of the solid acid and add 10 cc. of water: it will soon dissolve. To this add 5 cc. of strong solution of potassium hydroxide, and *at once* pour it into the funnel. Next hold the dish below the cork and open the pinchcock *p* a moment, to let the liquid run down and fill the tubes completely. Carefully take off the drop, which hangs at the lower end of the tube below the cork, with a piece of filter paper.

The Air. — Press the tube *t* up over the cork, as seen in Fig. 23, until the joint is air-tight, and after a minute put the rod *s* into the open hole of the cork. You have now imprisoned a tubeful of air; none can get out, and no more can get in.

The hole in the cork was left open, because, if it were not open, the pressure of the cork would crowd the air below, and there would be too much in the tube; and then, too, handling the tube warms it, and the volume of air changes with heat. With the hole open, the air in the tube soon comes to be just as warm and just as much

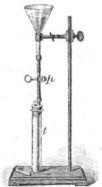

Fig. 23.

pressed as the air outside. Whenever a gas of any kind is to be measured, its *temperature* and *pressure* must be the *same as those of the air outside.*

The Absorption. — Now press the pinchcock *p ;* a little stream of the liquid falls into *t* at once, and then drops follow, or, if the tube be slightly inclined, a slender stream will flow down its side. It will continue to enter as long as there is any oxygen or carbon dioxide for it to absorb, and then stop. Close the pinchcock. The gas which is left in the tube is nitrogen.

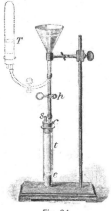

Fig. 24.

But this gas is crowded down by the pressure of the liquid in the rubber tube and funnel above ; and to relieve it from this pressure take hold of the cork *c*, and the rim of *t*, so as not to warm the gas with the hand, and lift the tube, bottom up, as shown at *T* in Fig. 24, making the level of the liquid the same in the tube and in the funnel. Then open the pinchcock. Some of the liquid will run out of *T*. When the liquid stands at the same level in the tube and in the funnel, close the cock and bring the tube down again.

The almost black liquid in *t* has now taken out all the oxygen and carbon dioxide from the tubeful of air, and left all its nitrogen.

The Measuring. — Measure the liquid in the tube to find how much oxygen was taken out,[1] and the space above it to find how much nitrogen was left.

To do this, slip two small rubber rings over the tube,

[1] And carbon dioxide also. But the volume of the carbon dioxide, in so small a quantity of air as we use in this experiment, is so little that we may leave it out of account.

and make the upper edge of one mark the place of the lower end of the cork; and of the other, the top of the liquid. These rings must not afterward be disturbed.

Now remove the cork, empty the tube, rinse it with water, and then let the last drop of water drain away. Finally, with a graduated cylinder, find out exactly how many cubic centimeters of water will fill the tube to the first ring; also how many cubic centimeters will fill the tube from the first to the second ring.

The Calculations. — From these two numbers we can find what part of the air is nitrogen, and what part is oxygen: for by their help we can answer the following questions, in their order, one after another, as shown by an example below.

How many cubic centimeters of air were in the tube at first?

How many cubic centimeters of nitrogen did this air yield?

How many cubic centimeters of oxygen did the same air yield?

Then what fractional part of the air is nitrogen?

What fractional part of the air is oxygen?

How many cubic centimeters of nitrogen in 100 cc. of air?

How many cubic centimeters of oxygen in 100 cc. of air?

An Example. — In an actual experiment it was found to take of

Water to fill the tube to the first ring	6.0 cc.
Water to fill the tube from the first to second ring . . .	23.5 cc.
Hence the number of cc. of air taken	29.5 cc.
The number of cc. of nitrogen found	23.5 cc.
The number of cc. of oxygen found	6.0 cc.

Now, this would show plainly that $\frac{23.5}{29.5}$ of the air is nitrogen, and $\frac{6.0}{29.5}$ of it is oxygen. Then in 100 cc. of air there would be

Nitrogen	79.66 cc.
Oxygen	20.34 cc.

XI. AMMONIA: THE COMPOUND OF NITROGEN AND HYDROGEN.

EXPERIMENT 54.

Object. — To obtain ammonia gas in small quantity.

Manipulation and Notes. — Powder a very little ammonium chloride and also a little good quicklime. Then mix them well, and put into a clean and dry test tube enough to half fill the rounded bottom. Take the tube between the fingers, with the thumb over its mouth, leaving a small opening at the lower edge, and hold it some time in the hot air above the flame, a little inclined, as shown in Fig. 25 (*note*).

Fig. 25.

Present a rod moistened with hydrochloric acid to the mouth of the tube.

Take the odor of the gas.

Introduce a strip of moist reddened litmus paper.

EXPERIMENT 55.

Object. — To obtain ammonia gas in larger quantity.

Method. — Decompose ammonium chloride by slaked lime, and collect by displacement of air.

Manipulation and Notes. — Set up three dry flasks, *a, b, c,* with all glass connections (Fig. 8, p. 20), with their short tubes toward the generator (a side-neck flask), and

5

join the long tube of c to a tube leading to the bottom of a bottle containing a very little water.

Mix *thoroughly* about 25 g. of powdered ammonium chloride with twice as much recently slaked lime *in fine dry powder*, and transfer to the generator. Heat with a very low flame. When the ammonia has driven the air all out of the receivers (decide by a rod wet with hydrochloric acid), lift the tube out of the bottle; twist its opened end upward; lower an inverted flask as far as possible over it, and fill this flask by displacement of air (*explain*). When the flask is filled, close it with a stopper, and stand it mouth down on the table. Disconnect the tube from flask c, and withdraw the heat.

EXPERIMENT 56.

Object. — *To discover properties of ammonia.*

Manipulation and Notes. — (*a*) What is its appearance? Note its odor. Is it heavier, or lighter, than air?

(*b*) Is it soluble in water? Take the flask which you filled by upward displacement of air; bring its mouth near the surface of water in a pan; remove the stopper and lower the mouth of the flask into the water.

Remove the flask with its contents, and place it on the table.

(*c*) What is its action on contact with flame? Disconnect flask c; invert it; remove its stopper; insert the flame of a taper.

(*d*) What is its action on litmus? Moisten two narrow strips of blue litmus paper. Redden one of them by holding it in the mouth of a bottle containing hydrochloric acid. Disconnect flask b. Open it, and at once insert the two papers. Describe effects. Is ammonia an acid, a basic, or a neutral substance?

(*e*) Is this character shown by a solution of the gas? Introduce a strip of reddened litmus paper into the solution in flask *c*. Or redden some blue litmus water with as little hydrochloric acid as will do it, and then pour into it some of the water which dissolved the gas in *c*.

Prepare a deep evaporating dish nearly full of reddened litmus water. Disconnect flask *a*. Invert it. Lower it nearly to the surface of the water. Remove its stopper, and press its mouth nearly to the bottom of the water. Describe and explain.

Tests. — How would you decide whether a given colorless gas is ammonia?

EXPERIMENT 57.

Object. — *To obtain ammonia from ammonium hydroxide.*

Manipulation and Notes. — Arrange the apparatus as in Fig. 26. Put 10 or 15 cc. of the ammonium hydroxide into the side-neck flask, close its mouth, and connect it with the short tube of the flask *a*, as shown. Now make the lamp flame very small, so that only a current of hot air will warm the liquid in the flask.

The gas obtained may be used for the purpose of studying the properties, as described in Exp. 56.

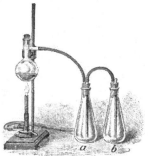

Fig. 26.

What is the difference between ammonia and ammonium hydroxide?

EXPERIMENT 58.

Object. — *To study the action of ammonium salts with potassium hydroxide.*

Manipulation and Notes. — Put a little solid ammonium chloride into a test tube. Moisten it with drops of potassium hydroxide, and heat it gently.

Examine the gas which is set free, (*a*) for odor, (*b*) with reddened litmus paper, (*c*) with hydrochloric acid on a glass rod.

Repeat the work, using ammonium sulphate, and again with ammonium carbonate.

Test. — How would you decide whether a given solid is a salt of ammonium?

EXPERIMENT 59.

Object. — *To ascertain the effect of heat on some ammonium salts.*

Manipulation and Notes. — Place a small quantity of the given salt in the bottom of a dry test tube. Apply heat gradually. Keep the upper part of the tube cold, and its mouth loosely closed with the finger.

Use (*a*) ammonium chloride, (*b*) ammonium carbonate, (*c*) ammonium nitrate. Test for gas in the tube, above the nitrate.

General. — Many salts of ammonium, like the chloride and the carbonate in these experiments, are vaporized without chemical change, by heat. Many others, like the nitrate, are decomposed by heat.

XII. NITRIC ACID, NITROGEN OXIDES, NITRATES.

EXPERIMENT 60.

Object. — *Is the action of nitric acid on metals similar to that of sulphuric acid?*

Manipulation and Notes. — Put a small piece of zinc into a test tube, and add 6 or 8 drops of nitric acid (*note*).

Recall the action of zinc on sulphuric acid (Exp. 7), or put a small piece of zinc in a test tube; cover it with dilute sulphuric acid, and test the gas.

Use a clipping of copper with nitric acid, and decide whether the action is the same as with zinc.

EXPERIMENT 61.

Object. — *To study the mutual action of nitric acid and copper.*

Manipulation and Notes. — (*a*) Fit up the apparatus for making and collecting gases heavier than air (Fig. 8, p. 20), using flasks *a*, *b*, *c*. Put water into both *a* and *b*, but none in *c*. After the connections are made, put about 7 g. of small pieces of copper into the side-neck flask, pour in about 40 cc. of dilute nitric acid (half water), and close the flask with its air-tight stopper (*note*). Is there any evidence that more than one kind of gas is produced?

(*b*) When the flask *c* is filled, disconnect *c*, attach a delivery tube to *b*, and proceed to collect the gas in a bottle by displacement of water. When the bottle is half full of gas, remove the tube from the water, disconnect the generator, and pour the *liquid* from it into an evaporating dish. Stand the dish, also the generator, aside until the end of the experiment.

(*c*) Proceed to examine the gases. Remove the stopper from *c* carefully, pour in gently a few cubic centimeters of water, and return the stopper to its place. Close the ends of both glass tubes; lift the flask and shake it well (*note*).

(*d*) Keep the tubes tightly closed while you immerse the mouth of the flask in water, then open them (*note*).

(*e*) Invert flask *b*, and let the water run out of the short tube. What must enter at the same time? Describe result, and account for it. Treat with water as you treated *c*.

(*f*) Lift the bottle just enough to let bubbles of air enter (*note*). Slip a glass plate under its mouth, lift and shake the bottle (*note*). Repeat these operations. How can these observed changes be explained?

(*g*) Very carefully open flask *a*, and insert a burning splinter (*note*).

End the Experiment. — Filter the liquid which came from the generator, and allow it to stand to evaporate. Put water in the generator, replace the stopper, cover the side neck, shake, and invert the side neck in water. Examine the residue in the dish after evaporation (*note*).

EXPERIMENT 62.

Object. — *To discover if the action with zinc is the same whether the acid is concentrated or dilute.*

Manipulation and Notes. — Make dilute nitric acid (1 of acid to 4 of water), and pour about 5 cc. upon a piece of zinc in a test tube. Keep it cool, and let it stand, loosely covered. Examine the gas liberated, comparing it with that obtained when the concentrated acid was used in Exp. 61, and with that given off by zinc and dilute sulphuric acid.

EXPERIMENT 63.

Object. — *To collect and examine the gas which zinc liberates from cold dilute nitric acid.*

Manipulation and Notes. — Arrange a side-neck flask with delivery tube, water pan, and bottle, to collect the gas by displacement of water (Fig. 11, p. 22). Dilute 25 cc. of nitric acid with 100 cc. of water. Put several pieces of zinc into the generator, and when the acid is cold pour it upon the zinc. Close the flask, wait a full minute, and then proceed at once to collect the gas. The generator should be kept cool; it may very well be supported in a dish of cold water. Finally take the tube from the water, and then test the gas with air and with flame.

Does it change by contact with air? Lift the bottle enough to let bubbles of air enter (*note*).

How does it act with flame? Open the generator, and apply the flame test in the usual way.

General. — There are several compounds of nitrogen and oxygen. One is a colorless gas which promotes combustion, called *nitrous oxide;* another is a colorless gas which extinguishes a taper flame, called *nitric oxide;* while another is a red-brown gas, called *nitrogen peroxide.*

What gas is set free when zinc or copper acts on *moderately strong* nitric acid? What other gas is produced when this one mixes with air (or oxygen)?

What gas is set free when zinc acts on *cold dilute* nitric acid?

EXPERIMENT 64.

Object. — *To study the action of zinc on very dilute nitric acid in presence of sulphuric acid.*

Manipulation and Notes. — Dilute 1 cc. of sulphuric acid with 5 cc. of water, and when cold pour it upon zinc in a test tube. *Keep it cold* by inserting it in cold water.

Test the gas. Add drop by drop a mixture of 1 cc. of nitric acid with 3 cc. of water, and observe its effect on the rapidity of the effervescence. Add the nitric acid until the effervescence ceases. Then let the tube stand for some hours.

Filter, and evaporate the liquid nearly to dryness. Transfer to a test tube, add drops of potassium hydroxide, and warm the mixture. Then test for odor, also with reddened litmus paper, also with hydrochloric acid on a glass rod, and decide what substance is liberated.

General. — The foregoing experiments show that the chemical action of zinc and nitric acid depends on temperature and the strength of the acid. In many other cases, as in this, the same substances yield different products, according to the conditions of the experiment.

EXPERIMENT 65.

Object. — *To learn the effect of heat on some nitrates.*

Manipulation and Notes. — Place a small quantity of the given nitrate in a dry test tube. Heat gradually. Examine the gas produced, and describe the effect of the heat.

Use (*a*) lead nitrate, (*b*) copper nitrate, (*c*) ammonium nitrate, or recall Exp. 59.

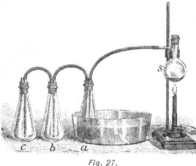

Fig. 27.

EXPERIMENT 66.

Object. — *To obtain nitrous oxide by heating ammonium nitrate.*

Manipulation and Notes. — Put from 7 to 10 g. of ammonium nitrate into the side-neck flask, which should be dry, and join the flasks, *a*, *b*, *c*, as usual for heavy gas. To condense steam, put the empty flask *a* into a dish of cold water (ice-water is best). It may be made to stand firmly in the water by a clamp. Use the gentle heat of a small flame, *only just hot enough* to melt and keep the nitrate bubbling.

What is the color of nitrous oxide? Its odor?

Test it in *b* with a spark on the end of a splinter. Leave *c* open for two or three minutes, and then test with a glowing splinter (*note*).

EXPERIMENT 67.

Object. — *To study the effect of nitric acid on ferrous sulphate, sometimes called "copperas."*

Manipulation and Notes. — (*a*) Into a little dilute nitric acid in a test tube drop a good crystal of the ferrous sulphate. Do not shake it. Describe the *color* which soon appears in the liquid around the crystal.

(*b*) Put 1 drop of strong acid into 5 cc. of water, and repeat the work with this very dilute acid.

(*c*) Try the solution of a nitrate, instead of nitric acid, in the same way. If you do not get the same result, there is probably little or no *free* nitric acid present.

(*d*) Mix a little solution of the nitrate with a solution of the ferrous sulphate, incline the tube, and let a little concentrated sulphuric acid run down the inside of the glass to the bottom. Do not shake it. Observe the effect where the two liquids are in contact.

(*e*) Make the experiment again with the nitrate and acid, but add the ferrous sulphate to the liquid when hot.

Test. — How would you decide whether a given liquid contains *free* nitric acid?

How would you decide whether a given solid is a nitrate?

Get a little of some white solid from the teacher, or a friend who knows what it is, and see if you can tell by the copperas test whether it is a nitrate.

XIII. CARBON, CARBON DIOXIDE, CARBONATES.

EXPERIMENT 68.

Object. — *To convert wood into charcoal.*

Manipulation and Notes. — Break the head from a match, and drop the body into a test tube. Then heat it slowly by holding the tube almost horizontally just above the tip of a lamp flame, and move the tube back and forth to heat the length of the wood. Describe all the products you can discover, noting particularly if vapors go off as gases, or condense into liquids. Compare the solid residue with a piece of soft-wood charcoal.

General. — This experiment illustrates the action involved in charcoal making.

EXPERIMENT 69.

Object. — *To examine the action of carbon on coloring substances.*

Manipulation and Notes. — (*a*) Prepare a filter, and rest the funnel in the mouth of a cylinder. Fill the filter nearly full of boneblack. Finally pour upon it some water colored with blue litmus. If it comes through still colored, pour it back, and let it run through a second time. Run it through a third time, if you think it best to do so (*note*).

(*b*) In the same way filter some water colored with cochineal (*note*).

(*c*) Try a solution of dark-brown sugar (*note*).

(*d*) Try a solution of potassium chromate. This is a mineral coloring matter; the others have been organic.

General. — These experiments reveal the power of certain forms of carbon as an absorbent, and illustrate its use as a filter for purifying water and refining sugar.

EXPERIMENT 70.

Object. — *To study the action of carbon on copper oxide.*

Manipulation and Notes. — Make a mixture of 1 g. of copper oxide with about its own bulk of powdered charcoal. Put it into the side - neck ignition tube, and place the end of the delivery tube in some lime-water contained in a test tube, as shown in Fig. 28, and then apply the heat of the Bunsen lamp.

From the effect on the limewater you recognize the product of

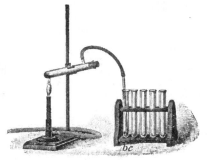

Fig. 28.

the action. From the residue in the tube you can judge the change in the oxide. You can then explain the action.

General. — This experiment reveals the power of carbon as a "reducing agent," which is applied in metallurgy to obtain metals from their ores.

EXPERIMENT 71.

Object. — *To obtain carbon dioxide and discover its properties.*

Manipulation and Notes. — Set up the apparatus shown in Fig. 29, long tubes toward generator. Water is placed in the bottle *d*, and in *a* enough to cover the end of the glass tube, while *b* contains a little limewater. The joints are all airtight.

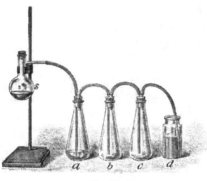

Fig. 29.

Slide with caution (*give reason*) several pieces of marble into the side-neck flask, and pour upon it about 25 cc. of dilute hydrochloric acid (half water), and at once close the flask with its stopper (*note*).

When the mutual action of the marble and the hydrochloric acid in the generator is nearly ended, study the gas as follows: Remove the tube from the bottle, and introduce a splinter flame (*note*).

(*a*) Is this gas heavier, or lighter, than air? When the bottle has stood uncovered for a little time, test with the flame again (*note*). For further evidence proceed to remove the stopper from flask *c*, and to hold the mouth of this flask upon the lip of a small wide-mouthed bottle, as if to pour the gas, as shown in Fig. 30. After a minute put a little limewater into the bottle; cover it with the hand, and shake it (*note*).

Fig. 30.

(*b*) Is this gas soluble in water? Put some limewater into a tube, and, without removing the stopper, pour a little of the water from flask *a* into it, as shown in Fig. 31. How does this result answer the question?

(*c*) How does the solution of this gas behave toward litmus? Put blue litmus water into a tube, and add the solution of gas from flask *a* (*note*). Is the solution basic, acid, or neutral?

(*d*) What is the effect of boiling the water solution of this gas? Pour a part of the water from the bottle *d* into blue litmus to decide whether it is a solution of this gas (*note*). Boil the remainder in a beaker for a few minutes, and then add it to another portion of blue litmus

Fig. 31.

to decide whether it is still a solution of the gas (*note*). Explain the difference in the two results.

General. — The foregoing experiments should reveal the chief characteristics of carbon dioxide (*name them*), and should enable you to distinguish this gas from all others.

EXPERIMENT 72.

Object. — *To test the mutual action of acids and carbonates.*

Manipulation and Notes. — Put some of the given carbonate into a test tube or beaker. Add dilute acid little by little. After the action has gone on for sufficient time, test the gas in the open vessel with a splinter flame.

Use (*a*) sodium carbonate and hydrochloric acid; (*b*) sodium carbonate and dilute sulphuric acid; (*c*) potassium carbonate and acetic acid; (*d*) calcium carbonate (marble) and dilute nitric acid.

General. — These experiments teach you how to identify a carbonate. How would you proceed?

EXPERIMENT 73.

Object. — To study the action of carbon dioxide on potassium hydroxide.

Manipulation and Notes. — To the delivery tube of a generator attach a glass tube through which gas may be carried into a strong solution of potassium hydroxide contained in a bottle. Pass carbon dioxide through the solution until no more is absorbed. Blow the gas out of the bottle. Then add hydrochloric acid (*note*). Insert a flame (*note*). What substance in the solution do you detect by these results ?

EXPERIMENT 74.

Object. — To ascertain whether the white precipitate made in limewater by carbon dioxide is a carbonate.

Manipulation and Notes. — Pass carbon dioxide through strong limewater. Filter the product and test the white precipitate with a little acid (*note and explain*).

General. — These experiments (73 and 74) are typical. Many other carbonates may be formed by the action of carbon dioxide on hydroxides.

XIV. COMBUSTION.

Preliminary. — Ordinary fuels are organic substances composed chiefly of carbon and hydrogen, with smaller proportions of oxygen, while some, such as wood and paper, contain a few other mineral substances. Remember that combustion is very rapid in oxygen alone, does not occur in nitrogen alone, and that the atmosphere consists chiefly of these two gases.

EXPERIMENT 75.

Object. — *To ascertain what substances are produced by the burning of a candle.*

Manipulation and Notes. — Obviously these products are in the form of vapors or gases (*explain*).

Bring a large, clean, and dry bottle down over the flame of a candle, and hold it there for a little while, as shown in Fig. 32.

Fig. 32.

When the action ceases (*give reason*), quickly place the bottle upright on the table, and cover it (*note*). One product is here suggested (*note*). Test the contents of the bottle with a small splinter flame (*note*). Leave the bottle awhile uncovered. Test again with flame (*note*). Test with limewater (*note*). Another product is now detected.

EXPERIMENT 76.

Object. — *To compare the products of combustion of other bodies with those of a candle.*

Manipulation and Notes. — Burn a splinter of wood, a small roll of paper, alcohol (by moistening a bit of cotton attached to a wire with the liquid), and a small jet of gas from the Bunsen lamp, in dry bottles, and examine the products in each case. Let no solid products escape notice.

General. — The foregoing experiments will enable you to *explain* the chemical changes in the combustion of fuels (*note*).

EXPERIMENT 77.

Object. — *To detect the carbon by which the carbon dioxide of a burning candle is produced.*

Manipulation and Notes. — Hold a square of clean dry window glass a short time across a candle flame just below the tip of it. Remove it before it becomes so hot as to break (*note*).

EXPERIMENT 78.

Object. — *To study the flame of the Bunsen lamp.*

Manipulation and Notes. — Close the holes in the tube of the burner, and describe the flame. Press a clean, dry, cold glass down upon it, flattening the tip (*note*).

Open the holes in the tube and describe the flame. Press the cold glass down upon it as before (*note*).

Which contains free carbon, — the luminous, or the non-luminous flame? In which case is the gas *mixed* with air before it burns? What would seem to be the source of the light in a luminous flame? Why is a good Bunsen flame smokeless?

EXPERIMENT 79.

Object. — *To examine the interior of a luminous flame.*

Manipulation and Notes. — (*a*) For this purpose the flame of an alcohol lamp is better than that of a candle, because it is larger. Lay the body of a match across the flame just above the wick, and leave it there only long enough for the flame to scorch it (*note*). Judge in what part of the flame the chemical action occurs (*note*).

(*b*) Press a square of paper down upon the flame almost to the tip of the wick, and remove it as soon as you see the upper surface scorch, and before the paper takes fire (*note*). In what part of the flame is the chemical action located ?

(*c*) Thrust the head of a match quickly into the interior of the flame just above the wick (*note*). Does combustion go on in the interior of a luminous flame ? You can give a reason.

EXPERIMENT 80.

Object. — *To study the combustion of charcoal in contact with hot potassium nitrate.*

Manipulation and Notes. — Put about 3 g. of potassium nitrate into a porcelain crucible, whose capacity is about 20 cc., and heat it by a Bunsen flame. You will learn whether it can be melted without decomposition (*note*). You will learn also whether it can be boiled without chemical change (*note*). When it boils, drop upon its surface a small splinter of charcoal (*note*).

Consider whether the burning charcoal gets its oxygen from the air in the crucible or from the nitrate, judging by the way it burned. Or you may try burning it in a crucible that contains no nitrate. Is the potassium nitrate an oxidizing agent ? Explain.

6

PART II.

REACTIONS AND PROPERTIES OF SOME COMPOUNDS OF METALS.

I. POTASSIUM (K), SODIUM (Na), AMMONIUM (NH_4).

EXPERIMENT 81.

Object. — *To study the mutual action of potassium and water.*

Manipulation and Notes. — Put about 100 cc. of water into a bottle. Drop into it a piece of potassium not larger than a small pea (CAUTION [1]), and cover it with a glass plate (*note*). Does the water show any evidence that a new substance is contained in it? Touch the tongue with a glass rod moistened with it. What does its taste suggest?

What is its action on litmus? Prepare two tubes, — one containing blue litmus, the other red litmus, — and pour some of the liquid into each (*note*). Is the product an acid, an hydroxide, or a neutral substance? Name it. Write and explain the reaction of the metal and water.

What would be produced by the action of carbon dioxide on the liquid in the bottle?

---

[1] Use a small piece, and stand at a little distance while the action goes on.

POTASSIUM, SODIUM, AMMONIUM.

EXPERIMENT 82.

Object. — *To obtain potassium carbonate from ashes.*

Manipulation and Notes. — Pack a filter of usual size about two thirds full of wood ashes. Pour hot water upon them to nearly fill the filter. Let it pass through. Pour the filtrate back upon the ashes. In this way repeat the filtration three or four times. Mention any qualities of the filtrate which you can detect. Test a small part of it with acid (*note*).

Finally evaporate the filtrate carefully to dryness (*note*). Prove that the residue contains a carbonate.

General. — This experiment illustrates the leaching process by which crude potassium carbonate is made on a large scale from wood ashes for use in arts and industries. From potassium carbonate many other salts of potassium are made.

EXPERIMENT 83.[1]

Object. — *To prepare potassium chloride from potassium carbonate.*

Manipulation and Notes. — Dissolve about 5 g. of K_2CO_3 in 50 cc. of water. Then add HCl slowly, until, after shaking it, the liquid will redden a bit of blue litmus paper. Finally evaporate the liquid to a small bulk and let it cool. Pour the liquid away from the crystals, and dry them on filter paper.

Why was the litmus paper used? What reaction took place? Prove that the product is a chloride. Keep this potassium chloride (KCl).

---

[1] Two or more of the following experiments may go on at once, and much time be thus saved which would otherwise be spent in *waiting.*

EXPERIMENT 84.

Object. — *To prepare potassium nitrate from potassium carbonate.*

Manipulation and Notes. — Proceed as directed in the preceding experiment, using nitric instead of hydrochloric acid. If the evaporation is carried far enough, you can watch the crystals growing in the liquid while it cools.

Write and explain the reaction. Prove that the product is a nitrate. Keep this potassium nitrate (KNO_3).

EXPERIMENT 85.

Object. — *To study the mutual action of sodium and water.*

Manipulation and Notes. — Put 100 cc. of water into a wide-mouthed bottle. Drop in upon it a piece of sodium as large as a small pea. Cover the bottle with a glass plate (*note*).

Test the gas in the bottle with a splinter flame (*note*). Point out any apparent difference between this action of sodium and that of potassium on water.

Test for the taste of the liquid (*note*). Test the action of the liquid with litmus, and decide whether the product of the action is an acid, an hydroxide, or a neutral substance.

EXPERIMENT 86.

Object. — *To convert sodium carbonate into other salts of sodium.*

Manipulation and Notes. — Follow the directions given in Exps. 83 and 84 for the preparation of salts of potassium. In each case write and explain the reaction, and name the salt produced.

Use (*a*) hydrochloric acid, (*b*) nitric acid, (*c*) sulphuric acid.

EXPERIMENT 87.

Object. — *To convert ammonium carbonate into other ammonium salts.*

Manipulation and Notes. — Proceed as directed in the preparation of potassium salts. Use (*a*) hydrochloric acid, (*b*) nitric acid.

General. — The foregoing experiments show a very marked chemical resemblance between potassium and sodium (*explain*), and between the salts of potassium, sodium, and ammonium (*explain*).

EXPERIMENT 88.

Object. — *To study the action of heat on salts of potassium, sodium, and ammonium.*

Manipulation and Notes. — Place a very small quantity of the given salt in a porcelain dish, and heat it gradually. Describe the change, and finally point out any marked difference between the three classes of salts.

Use (*a*) the carbonates, (*b*) the chlorides.

EXPERIMENT 89.

Object. — *To study the action of potassium, sodium, and ammonium salts on flame.*

Manipulation and Notes. — Bend one end of a piece of platinum wire into a round loop about as large as this O. Moisten this loop, and plunge it into the salt to be tested. A little of the salt will cling to the wire. Hold it in the mantle of a colorless flame, as in Fig. 33 (*note*).

Fig. 33.

Look at this colored flame through a piece of cobalt-blue glass (*note*).

After each trial, thoroughly wash and heat the loop before using it with another salt.

(*a*) For potassium salts use the chloride, the nitrate, and the carbonate (*note*).

The color will sometimes come more surely if the loop is moistened with hydrochloric acid. Try potassium carbonate without hydrochloric acid, and then with it (*note*).

(*b*) For sodium salts use the chloride moistened, the nitrate, and the carbonate without and with hydrochloric acid (*note*).

(*c*) For ammonium salts use the chloride, the nitrate, or sulphate, or carbonate (*note*).

(*d*) Make a mixture of a sodium and a potassium salt, and burn the mixture on the platinum loop. Which color can you get with the naked eye? Which if you look through cobalt glass?

General. — The two preceding experiments reveal some well-marked differences in the actions of potassium, sodium, and ammonium salts, by which one should be able to decide whether a given salt belongs to one or another of these classes.

For the potassium hydroxide test for ammonium salts, see Exp. 58.

Non-volatile compounds cannot color flames (*give reason*).

For practice, prove the salts prepared in Exp. 84 to be potassium salts, those in Exp. 86 to be sodium salts, those in Exp. 87 to be ammonium salts. Try other specimens also.

II. CALCIUM (Ca), BARIUM (Ba), STRONTIUM (Sr).

EXPERIMENT 90.

Object. — *To convert calcium carbonate into calcium chloride.*

Manipulation and Notes. — Reduce a small piece of marble to coarse powder, and add it little by little to 5 cc. of hydrochloric acid in a test tube (*note*). What is the escaping gas? Can any solid product be seen in the liquid? Write the reaction which should be expected between the two substances used, and judge thereby what product should be in the liquid. Evaporate the liquid. Do you find the suspected substance? Why, then, did it not appear in the liquid? To answer this last question, try the solubility of the product in water.

EXPERIMENT 91.

Object. — *To convert calcium chloride into calcium carbonate.*

Manipulation and Notes. — Place about 5 cc. of calcium chloride in a test tube, add about as much water, and heat the mixture to boiling point (*give reason*). Then add slowly a solution of ammonium carbonate as long as it continues to produce the precipitate. To know when to stop, let the solid settle a little, and then notice whether another drop of the ammonium carbonate has any effect (*note*). The white precipitate is calcium carbonate. Why does it appear as a precipitate? To answer this question, try the solubility of calcium carbonate in water.

Write the reaction, and decide what else was probably produced. Why was not this substance also precipitated?

Is there any *calcium* compound left in the liquid? This should teach you how to get all the calcium out of any liquid which contains its salts in solution. You can also give the reason why no precipitates were obtained in the experiments with potassium, sodium, and ammonium salts.

EXPERIMENT 92.

Object. — *To compare the reactions of calcium, barium, and strontium salts.*

Manipulation and Notes. — (*a*) Arrange three tubes, each with 5 cc. of water, and add to one 5 cc. of a solution of calcium chloride ($CaCl_2$); to the second, 5 cc. of solution of barium chloride ($BaCl_2$); to the third, 5 cc. of solution of strontium chloride ($SrCl_2$). Then add to each, drops of ammonium carbonate, $(NH_4)_2CO_3$ (*note*). Point out the resemblances of these products to one another. Write the reactions, and note their great similarity.

(*b*) Use solutions of the nitrates of these metals, and proceed as in (*a*).

(*c*) Use the chlorides; add NH_4Cl to the solutions; then add the $(NH_4)_2CO_3$. Does the presence of NH_4Cl hinder the production of the precipitate?

(*d*) Try to dissolve a little of the precipitate in NH_4OH (*note*).

General. — All the corresponding compounds of these three metals exhibit very close resemblances, and their reactions throughout are similar.

EXPERIMENT 93.

Object. — *To study some differences in the reactions of barium, calcium, and strontium salts.*

Manipulation and Notes. — (*a*) The reaction with $CaSO_4$. Arrange three test tubes, each with 5 cc. of water, and add to one 5 cc. of *strong* solution of $BaCl_2$, to the second as much *strong* solution of $SrCl_2$, and to the third as much *strong* solution of $CaCl_2$. Then add to each a little solution of calcium sulphate ($CaSO_4$). Note whether precipitates are formed at once in the cold solutions. Heat, to boiling, those in which no precipitate has appeared (*note*). Point out the difference in the behavior of the Ba, Sr, and Ca salts in this reaction.

(*b*) The flame coloration. Follow directions given for the flame test in Exp. 89. Use the chlorides (*note*). Use the carbonates (*note*). Use the carbonates moistened with HCl (*note*). Observe the flames through cobalt glass (*note*). Point out the difference between these and the flame colors of potassium and sodium.

General. — By the peculiarities revealed in the foregoing experiment you should be able to distinguish the Ba, Sr, and Ca compounds from one another, and also from those of K, Na, and NH_4.

For practice, examine substances which may be given by the instructor, and try to decide whether each one is a compound of Ca, Sr, or Ba.

III. MAGNESIUM (Mg).

EXPERIMENT 94.

Object. — *To study the reactions of soluble magnesium compounds with ammonium carbonate.*

Manipulation and Notes. — (*a*) Arrange two tubes, each with about 5 cc. of water. Add to one tube about 5 cc., and to the other about $\frac{1}{2}$ cc., of magnesium chloride ($MgCl_2$). Heat the strong solution, and add ammonium carbonate ($NH_4)_2CO_3$ (*note*). Treat the weak solution in the same way (*note*).

The product obtained from the strong solution is magnesium carbonate ($MgCO_3$), which is insoluble in water; but in weak solution the product is double carbonate of magnesium and ammonium ($MgCO_3(NH_4)_2CO_3$), which is soluble.

(*b*) Is $MgCO_3$ soluble in NH_4Cl? To answer this question, transfer *a little* of the carbonate obtained from strong solution to another tube, and add considerable NH_4Cl.

(*c*) Can the precipitate be obtained in presence of much NH_4Cl? Mix 5 cc. of NH_4Cl with 5 cc. of $MgCl_2$, and then add the ($NH_4)_2CO_3$. Why is no precipitate formed?

Write the reaction which occurred in (*a*). You can judge from this reaction, in the light of (*b*) and (*c*), whether you should ever expect to precipitate *all* the magnesium in a solution by means of ammonium carbonate (*note*).

(*d*) Is $MgCO_3$ soluble in NH_4OH? Try a little of the precipitate with NH_4OH, as you did with NH_4Cl in (*b*) (*note*). Would NH_4OH prevent the precipitation of the carbonate, as did NH_4Cl? Would HCl prevent the precipitation of the carbonate? Why?

IV. ZINC (Zn).

EXPERIMENT 95.

Object. — *To study the reaction of ammonium carbonate with soluble compounds of zinc.*

Manipulation and Notes. — Use zinc chloride ($ZnCl_2$). Add a few drops of solution of $ZnCl_2$ to 10 cc. of water, and then add $(NH_4)_2CO_3$ (*note*).

Write the reaction, and name the zinc product.

Ascertain whether NH_4Cl will prevent the foregoing result, as it does the similar reaction with $MgCl_2$.

EXPERIMENT 96.

Object. — *To study the reaction of ammonium hydroxide with zinc chloride.*

Manipulation and Notes. — To a few cubic centimeters of the $ZnCl_2$ mixed with an equal bulk of water, add NH_4OH little by little (*note*). Continue to add the hydroxide, until after shaking it, and then blowing the air out of the tube, the strong odor of ammonia remains (*note*).

Write the reaction and name the zinc product. This compound of zinc is insoluble in water, but it is soluble in ammonium hydroxide. Does this explain the results just now obtained ?

When a precipitate is dissolved by the reagent which produces it, it is said to be *soluble in excess.*

EXPERIMENT 97.

Object. — *To study the reaction of zinc chloride with hydrogen sulphide.*

Manipulation and Notes. — (*a*) Put about 4 cc. of strong solution of H_2S into a tube, and add a solution of $ZnCl_2$ drop by drop (*note*).

(*b*) Repeat the experiment, varying it by adding a drop of HCl to the chloride, so that the $ZnCl_2$ is in an *acid* solution (*note*).

(*c*) Repeat the experiment, varying it by making the zinc chloride *alkaline* by adding drops of NH_4OH until the hydroxide formed at first is dissolved in excess (*note*).

Write the reaction of $ZnCl_2$ with H_2S.

What is the action of the HCl in (*b*)?

What is the action of the NH_4OH in (*c*)?

(*d*) To 10 cc. of water add drops of $ZnCl_2$, and then a drop or two of ammonium sulphide (NH_4HS). Compare the product with the sulphide obtained in (*c*). Write the reaction.

General. — The foregoing experiment has shown what reagents may be used to convert any soluble compound of zinc into zinc sulphide (*explain*); the condition necessary in order to obtain the sulphide as a precipitate (*explain*); its color, and something about its solubility in water, in acids, and in hydroxides.

Suggestion. — Instead of using H_2S in solution to produce the sulphide of metals, the gas itself will be found much more active, and much more satisfactory in every respect but one; and that is, the difficulty in using the gas without suffering from its odor. A generator large enough to supply the gas for all, and fixed in a good ventilating chamber, may be used. Or, if a student can be trusted to be steadfastly careful, he may use a small gas apparatus consisting of a side-neck tube generator, and three small wide-mouthed bottles, *a*, *b*, *c*, in place of the usual conical flasks, with long tubes toward generator. The bottle *a* may be moderately packed with cotton wool, or contain a little water, to intercept substances carried over by the gas. In *b* the solution to be treated should be placed, and *c* should contain dilute ammonium hydroxide (half water) to absorb the excess of gas which would otherwise poison the atmosphere.

For each experiment, ferrous sulphide (only enough for the experiment) should be put into the generator. Acid, made so dilute that a steady but *slow* stream of gas is evolved, should be added. All joints should be tight; and the generator should exhaust itself before *b* is removed. Remove *b* by slipping it from the stopper, and then let the apparatus stand ready for the next call upon it. The ammonia in *c* will need changing only when it has become yellow.

V.   CADMIUM   (Cd).

EXPERIMENT 98.

Object. — *To study the reaction of cadmium chloride with ammonium carbonate.*

Manipulation and Notes. — Use a solution of cadmium chloride ($CdCl_2$), and follow the directions given in Exp. 94 (*note*).

EXPERIMENT 99.

Object. — *To study the reaction of cadmium chloride with ammonium hydroxide.*

Manipulation and Notes. — Follow the directions given in Exp. 96 (*note*).

EXPERIMENT 100.

Object. — *To study the reaction of cadmium chloride with hydrogen sulphide.*

Manipulation and Notes. — Adopt the plan given in detail in Exp. 97, (*a*), (*b*), (*c*), (*d*), discussing all the results as fully as you can.

Compare the sulphides of cadmium and zinc.

A.   Exercise in Collecting and Tabulating Results of Experiments.

Object. — *To compare the carbonates of barium, strontium, calcium, magnesium, zinc, potassium, sodium, and ammonium.*

Prepare a skeleton table like that on p. 95.   In the first column put the symbols of the metals whose carbonates are to be compared. In the second column put the formulas of the carbonates. Head the following columns with the particular facts in regard to which you wish to compare them. Consult your notes of the experiments you made with each, and state the fact for each in its proper blank. If, in any case, your experiments have not revealed the fact directly, nor enabled you to *infer it* with certainty, leave the blank unfilled. If your experiment has revealed no change, show this by a dash drawn in the blank.

Table: Comparison of Properties of some Carbonates.

METALS.	CARBON-ATES.	COLOR.	SOL'Y IN H_2O	SOL'Y IN HCl	SOL'Y IN NH_4Cl	SOL'Y IN NH_4OH
Ba	Ba CO_3	White.	Insol.	Soluble to Ba Cl_2	Insol.	Insol.
Sr						
Ca						
Mg						
Zn						
K						
Na						
NH_4						

By what reagent may the soluble compounds of Ca be converted into $CaCO_3$? (Exp. 91.)

In what respect do the carbonates of K, Na, and NH_4 differ from all the others, and resemble one another? What does the table show in regard to the carbonates of Ba, Sr, Ca? In what respects is $MgCO_3$ related to those of Ba, Sr, Ca? Wherein does it differ?

If a solution contains the six metals, Ba, Sr, Ca, K, Na, and NH_4. in the form of chlorides, by what reagent could you precipitate three of them in the form of carbonates, and leave the other three in solution?

VI. MERCURY (Hg).

EXPERIMENT 101.

Object. — *To study the reaction of mercury with nitric acid.*

Manipulation and Notes. — (*a*) Into one tube, *a*, put a small globule of mercury; into another tube, *b*, put a small globule of the same metal. To the metal in tube *a* add 1 cc. of dilute nitric acid (*note*), and let stand in the rack until action ceases. To the metal in tube *b* add 1 cc. of moderately strong nitric acid, and apply heat (*note*). What salt of mercury is probably produced in the tubes?

(*b*) To 5 cc. of water add drops of the clear liquid in tube *a*, and then add drops of HCl (*note*). To 5 cc. of water add drops of clear liquid from tube *b*, and then drops of HCl (*note*). If you get the same results, you are entitled to say that the same salt is made by the nitric acid in both tubes: is it so?

(*c*) Take the clear liquid from *a*, and heat it to boiling. Add a drop or two of concentrated nitric acid, and boil again. Put drops of this liquid into 5 cc. of water, and add HCl (*note*). Compare with results in *b*. You can now judge whether this liquid contains the same salt it contained before boiling with HNO_3.

General. — This study should reveal the fact that mercury is capable of yielding two salts with nitric acid. We have mercurous nitrate ($Hg_2(NO_3)_2$) in tube *a*, and mercuric nitrate ($Hg(NO_3)_2$) in tube *b*.

This twofold action of mercury is general. There are two classes of mercury compounds.

(*d*) Is mercurous chloride soluble in water? To 10 cc. of water add a few drops of mercurous nitrate, and then HCl drop by drop, carefully, until a drop produces no change. Do not add excess. The tube now contains the chloride mixed with water. Transfer a little to another tube, add more water, and shake vigorously. In this way you can judge whether it is soluble in *cold* water. Heat the mixture and judge whether it is soluble in *hot* water.

(*e*) Is mercurous chloride affected by NH_4OH? Treat the chloride remaining from (*d*) with drops of NH_4OH (*note*).

EXPERIMENT 102.

Object. — *To study the effect of ammonium hydroxide on soluble mercurous and mercuric compounds.*

Manipulation and Notes. — Add a few drops of strong solution of the given compound to 5 cc. of water, and then add the NH_4OH drop by drop to excess (Exp. 96).

Use (*a*) solution of mercurous nitrate (*note*), (*b*) solution of mercuric chloride (*note*).

General. — The actions of HCl on mercurous and mercuric compounds, generally, are the same as upon the two nitrates in (*b*), Exp. 101. The actions of NH_4OH on mercurous nitrate and mercuric chloride are also typical of its action on the *ous* and the *ic* compounds generally. You can use these reactions to decide whether a given substance is a mercurous or a mercuric compound (*explain*).

EXPERIMENT 103.

Object. — *To study the reaction of compounds of mercury with hydrogen sulphide.*

Manipulation and Notes. — (*a*) Use mercurous nitrate, and proceed as directed in (*a*), Exp. 97 (*note*).

7

(*b*) Use mercuric chloride, and proceed in the same way (*note*). What differences, if any, can you discover in the two experiments? What differences in the two sulphides produced?

(*c*) Use mercuric chloride in *acid* solution.

(*d*) Use mercuric chloride in alkaline solution. Add drops of NH_4OH (*note*), then treat it with the H_2S (*note, explain*).

(*e*) Use dilute solution of $HgCl_2$, and treat it with ammonium sulphide, as in Exp. 97 (*d*).

(*f*) Is this sulphide soluble in HNO_3? To answer this question, proceed as follows: First obtain the clean sulphide. For this purpose filter it out of the liquid, and then *wash it* by pouring water into the filter, enough to cover the sulphide, letting it run through, and repeating the operation. Remove the filter from the funnel, open it out, and lay the paper flat upon a glass plate. Then with a spatula transfer a very little of the sulphide from the paper to a porcelain dish; cover it with dilute HNO_3, and stir it with a glass rod. If it do not dissolve in the cold, apply a gentle heat. If it do not dissolve in the hot dilute acid, try concentrated acid in the same way.

EXPERIMENT 104.

Object. — *To liberate metallic mercury from mercurous chloride.*

Manipulation and Notes. — Use a bright piece of copper wire. Acidify a dilute solution of the chloride with a drop of HCl, and insert a piece of bright copper wire. After a little time observe the coating on the wire. Its appearance, especially after being rubbed with a cloth, will be likely to inform you what this coating is. Mercury is volatile: test this coating by heating the wire (*note*).

VII. SILVER (Ag).

EXPERIMENT 105.

Object. — *To study the reaction of silver nitrate with hydrochloric acid.*

Manipulation and Notes. — (*a*) To 10 cc. of water add 4 or 5 drops of $AgNO_3$, and then drops of HCl (*note*). Shake it vigorously (*note*). Write the reaction.

(*b*) Is silver chloride soluble in hot water? Put a little of that just made into a little water in another tube, and heat to boiling.

(*c*) Is this chloride affected by NH_4OH? Transfer a little to another tube, and add drops of NH_4OH.

(*d*) How is it affected by light? Recall the result of a former experiment, or expose the remainder of the chloride made in (*a*) to direct sunlight.

EXPERIMENT 106.

Object. — *To convert silver nitrate into silver sulphide.*

Manipulation and Notes. — (*a*) Pass H_2S through a dilute solution of $AgNO_3$, or add drops of the $AgNO_3$ solution to 5 cc. of the solution of H_2S in water (*note*). Write the reaction.

(*b*) To a dilute solution of $AgNO_3$ add drops of ammonium sulphide in slight excess. An excess will be present when the liquid retains the odor of this reagent, or if, when the precipitate settles sufficiently, you can detect the color of the reagent in the liquid (*note*). Write the reaction. What evidence that the same sulphide is obtained in (*a*) and (*b*)?

EXPERIMENT 107.

Object. — *To liberate metallic silver from silver nitrate.*

Manipulation and Notes. — (*a*) Use a bright piece of copper, as in Exp. 104, omitting the HCl (*give reason*). Observe the coating which gathers on the wire: it is metallic silver.

(*b*) Use a globule of mercury. Put the globule into a little dish, and cover it with concentrated solution of $AgNO_3$, and let it stand.

VIII. COPPER (Cu).

EXPERIMENT 108.

Object. — *To ascertain the action of hydrochloric acid with soluble compounds of copper.*

Manipulation and Notes. — Use dilute solution of copper sulphate ($CuSO_4$). Add 1 cc. of the copper-sulphate solution to 10 cc. of water, and half as much hydrochloric acid, drop by drop (*note*).

Has the sulphate been converted into the chloride? To answer this question, evaporate the liquid to crystallization, and, after rinsing the crystals in water to rid them of any trace of HCl, dissolve in water; then decide whether the substance is a chloride by means of $AgNO_3$, followed by NH_4OH (Exp. 38 (*a*) (*c*)), or a sulphate by means of $BaCl_2$ (Exp. 48).

What property of $CuCl_2$ makes it impossible to obtain it *as a precipitate* from any solution by means of HCl?

EXPERIMENT 109.

Object. — *To study the preparation and properties of copper sulphide.*

1. To Obtain the Sulphide.

Manipulation and Notes. — (*a*) Add about 1 cc. of dilute solution of copper sulphate ($CuSO_4$) to 10 cc. of H_2S solution; or, better, pass the hydrogen-sulphide gas through the mixture until it is saturated (*note*).[1]

---

[1] If the gas is used in (*a*), the work in (*b*), (*c*), and (*d*) can go on with the H_2S solution while the gas is saturating the liquid. In this way time may be saved.

(*b*) Acidulate a solution of $CuSO_4$ with HCl, and treat it with the H_2S solution or gas (*note*).

(*c*) Add a drop or two of NH_4OH to a solution of $CuSO_4$, and then treat the mixture with H_2S (*note*).

By these trials you learn whether the sulphide is precipitated equally well in neutral, acid, or alkaline solution.

Notice that $NH_4OH + H_2S = H_2O + NH_4HS$.

(*d*) To 10 cc. of water add 1 cc. of $CuSO_4$, and then a few drops of ammonium sulphide (NH_4HS) (*note*). Judge from the results in (*b*) and (*c*) whether the one reagent (ammonium sulphide) may be used instead of the two (NH_4OH and H_2S together) for the same result.

Write and explain the reactions in (*a*) and (*d*).

2. To Discover some Properties of Copper Sulphide.

Manipulation and Notes. — (*a*) What is the color of this sulphide? Recall any sulphides previously seen which resemble this one ; also others which are quite different.

(*b*) Is this CuS soluble in HCl?

(*c*) Is this CuS soluble in HNO_3?

(*d*) Is this CuS soluble in yellow ammonium sulphide?[1]

EXPERIMENT 110.

Object. — *To learn the action of ammonium hydroxide with a soluble compound of copper.*

Manipulation and Notes. — Mix 1 cc. of solution of $CuSO_4$ with 10 cc. of water, and add NH_4OH by drops, shaking the tube well after each drop. Note the effect of the first drop, then of additional drops, and finally of excess.

---

[1] The solution of ammonium sulphide, prepared by saturating NH_4OH with H_2S, gradually becomes yellow. In this condition, it contains more than one ammonium sulphide; and among them is the $(NH)_2S$, which is a more powerful solvent than NH_4HS.

EXPERIMENT 111.

Object. — *To liberate the copper from a soluble compound of this metal.*

Manipulation and Notes. — Add 1 cc. of dilute solution of the given compound (say, $CuSO_4$) to 10 cc. of water, and insert a bright piece of iron, — a wire, a knife blade or a nail (*note*).

A drop of HCl may facilitate the action.

Write and explain the reaction.

EXPERIMENT 112.

Object. — *To prove that a dime contains copper and silver.*

Manipulation and Notes. — Upon a dime in a porcelain dish pour 10 cc. of nitric acid, half water, and warm it, if necessary, to start the chemical action (*note*). When the action is over, pour 2 cc. of the solution into 10 cc. of water, and add solution of sodium chloride as long as it has any effect (*note*). Filter, and wash the precipitate three times with water.

Then prove that the filtrate contains copper by using iron as in Exp. 111, and that the precipitate contains silver, which you can do by showing (Exp. 105 (*b*) (*c*)) that it is silver chloride.

IX. LEAD (Pb).

EXPERIMENT 113.

Object. — *To ascertain the action of hydrochloric acid with soluble compounds of lead.*

Manipulation and Notes. — (*a*) Use a dilute solution of lead nitrate ($PbNO_3$), and treat it as $AgNO_3$ was treated in Exp. 105 (*a*) (*note*).

Next use a strong solution of the $PbNO_3$ in the same way (*note*).

What is the precipitate? Write and explain the reaction. Why, probably, did it not appear in the dilute solution?

(*b*) Is this chloride soluble in hot water? Heat the mixture obtained in (*a*) to boiling (*note*). Let the solution stand until cold. In what form does the chloride reappear?

(*c*) Is there any chloride held in solution by cold water? When the tube has become quite cold, decant the clear liquid and evaporate it almost to dryness.

(*d*) Learn the effect of NH_4OH on the precipitate of $PbCl_2$ by the process in Exp. 105 (*c*).

(*e*) Learn the effect of light on this chloride, Exp. 105 (*d*).

EXPERIMENT 114.

Object. — *To study the preparation and properties of lead sulphide.*

1. To Obtain the Sulphide.

Manipulation and Notes. — (*a*) Use lead nitrate or lead acetate, and follow directions for CuS in Exp. 109, 1 (*a*).

(*b*) Learn whether the same result may be obtained in an acid solution of the lead compound. Follow directions given in Exp. 109, 1 (*b*).

(*c*) Learn whether the same result may be obtained in an alkaline solution of the lead compound. Follow directions given in Exp. 109, 1 (*c*).

(*d*) Learn whether you can obtain the sulphide by the use of ammonium sulphide.

2. TO DISCOVER THE PROPERTIES OF LEAD SULPHIDE.

Manipulation and Notes. — (*a*) Obtain the clean sulphide for examination. Filter and wash the precipitate as directed in Exp. 103 (*f*).

(*b*) What is the color of this sulphide? Can you distinguish it by its appearance from CuS? CdS? HgS? ZnS?

(*c*) Is this PbS soluble in HCl?

(*d*) Is this sulphide soluble in HNO_3?

(*e*) Is lead sulphide soluble in ammonium sulphide?

EXPERIMENT 115.

Object. — *To learn the action of ammonium hydroxide with a soluble compound of lead.*

Manipulation and Notes. — Use a solution of lead nitrate $(Pb(NO_3)_2)$ or of lead acetate $(Pb(C_2H_3O_2)_2)$, and follow directions found in Exp. 110.

EXPERIMENT 116.

Object. — *To liberate lead from a soluble compound of the metal.*

Manipulation and Notes. — Use the acetate. Add a drop of HCl; insert a strip of clean zinc, and let it stand, to be observed at intervals until you can describe the result.

Write the reaction, and compare it with those in the liberation of Hg, Ag, and Cu.

Or make the experiment on a larger scale, and obtain the so-called "lead-tree," as follows : —

Dissolve 8 or 10 g. of lead acetate, commonly called "sugar of lead," in about 500 cc. of water, and, if the solution is cloudy, add a little acetic acid to clear it. Put this solution into a white glass bottle, and then hang in it a strip of clean sheet zinc (Fig. 34), and let it stand undisturbed until the next day, when you will be able to describe the beautiful growth of crystals which has long been called the "lead-tree."

Fig. 34.

EXPERIMENT 117.

Object. — *To obtain lead iodide.*

Manipulation and Notes. — Add drops of a solution of potassium iodide (KI) to a moderately dilute solution of lead nitrate (Pb $(NO_3)_2$) (*note*). Write the reaction.

Heat the contents of the tube (*note*). If the iodide is visible after heating to boiling, add a little water and heat again. Let the solution cool spontaneously (*note*). Explain the changes.

B.   Exercise in Collecting and Tabulating Results of Experiments.

Object. — *To compare the properties of the chlorides of silver, mercury, copper, and lead.*

Prepare a skeleton table like that on p. 107. Fill the blanks by gleaning the facts from your own notes, as directed in Exercise **A**, p. 94.

Table: Comparison of Properties of some Chlorides.

METALS.	CHLO-RIDES.	COLOR.	SOL'Y IN H$_2$O COLD. HOT.	SOL'Y IN H Cl	EFFECT OF NH$_4$OH	EFFECT OF LIGHT.
Ag						
Hg$_2$						
Hg						
Cu						
Pb	Pb Cl$_2$	White.	Slightly—Freely.	Insol.	———	

In what respects are the chlorides of Ag, Hg$_2$, and Pb alike ?   In what respects do the chlorides of Hg and Cu differ from the other three ?

In what respects do the two chlorides of mercury differ ? Can you find out whether a given solution contains a compound of Hg$_2$?

If a solution contains all these metals in the form of nitrates, by what reagent can you precipitate the Ag, Hg$_2$, and Pb in the form of chlorides, and leave the others in solution ?

Having a precipitate consisting of chlorides, how can you learn whether PbCl$_2$ is present ?   By what reagent can you decide whether Hg$_2$Cl$_2$ is present in such a precipitate ?

X. TIN (Sn).

EXPERIMENT 118.

Object. — To study the reaction of tin with hydrochloric acid.

Manipulation and Notes. — Place 5 cc. of strong hydrochloric acid in a test tube, and drop into it a piece of granulated tin. Then heat until the effervescence is brisk; after which keep the tube warm by holding it above the flame of the lamp, until, when taken away from the heat, the bubbling nearly or quite stops. If, before this occurs, the tin is used up, another piece must be added. When the effervescence is brisk, test the escaping gas with a match flame.

What gas is set free by the action, and into what compound is the tin changed? Write the reaction.

EXPERIMENT 119.

Object. — To ascertain the effect of nitric acid on the solution of tin chloride obtained in the previous experiment.

Manipulation and Notes. — (*a*) Pour about 2 cc. of the $SnCl_2$ solution into another tube, add four or five *drops* of strong nitric acid, and boil the mixture a minute. Is there any evidence of a chemical change?

(*b*) Prove that a chemical change has or has not been made by the HNO_3. This may be done by trying the liquid with mercuric chloride before and after boiling with HNO_3. Identical results would show that no change had been produced.

Prepare two clean tubes with 10 cc. of water in each, and

add to one about 1 cc. of the solution[1] of the tin chloride of Exp. 118, and to the other about as much of the solution after its treatment with HNO_3 in Exp. 119. Next add a drop of a solution of mercuric chloride to the first (*note*). Add drop by drop more mercuric chloride (*note*).

Now add to the other solution drops of mercuric-chloride solution in the same way (*note*).

From these results you can judge whether the tin chloride was changed by the HNO_3.

Is it still a chloride? To answer this question, test a portion of the solution with $AgNO_3$, and add NH_4OH, Exp. 38 (*a*) (*c*).

General. — The foregoing work should reveal the fact that tin is capable of yielding two chlorides. We have stannous chloride ($SnCl_2$) and stannic chloride ($SnCl_4$). Mercuric chloride enables us to distinguish one from the other, as it is reduced to gray mercury by the former only. This twofold character of tin is general; there are two classes of tin compounds.

EXPERIMENT 120.

Object. — *To precipitate and study the properties of the tin sulphides.*

1. To PRECIPITATE THE SULPHIDES.

Manipulation and Notes. — To 10 cc. of water add $\frac{1}{2}$ cc. of the stannous chloride obtained in Exp. 118; and again, to 10 cc. of water add $\frac{1}{2}$ cc. of the stannic chloride of Exp. 119. Then pass hydrogen sulphide through both to saturation (*note*).

The first gives stannous sulphide (SnS).

The second gives stannic sulphide (SnS_2).

---

[1] A white precipitate may appear at this point. If so, the addition of a little HCl will dissolve it. If the solution already contains sufficient excess of HCl, the precipitate will not appear.

2. To Discover some Properties of Tin Sulphides.

Manipulation and Notes. — (*a*) Obtain the clean sulphides for examination. To do this, follow the directions found in Exp. 103 (*f*).

Note their marked difference in color, and recall other sulphides which they resemble.

(*b*) Are these sulphides soluble in HCl? Exp. 103 (*f*).

(*c*) Are these sulphides soluble in HNO_3?

(*d*) Are these sulphides soluble in yellow ammonium sulphide?

General. — If a given solution contains a compound of copper or of tin, how will you convert that compound into a sulphide? Will the sulphide remain in solution, or be obtained as a precipitate? Why? Can you judge by its appearance whether it is a copper sulphide or a tin sulphide? Can you decide with certainty?

EXPERIMENT 121.

Object. — *To study the reaction of soluble tin compounds with ammonium hydroxide.*

Manipulation and Notes. — Use solutions of (*a*) stannous chloride made in Exp. 118; (*b*) stannic chloride made in Exp. 119 (*a*). Follow directions found in Exp. 96.

XI. ARSENIC (As), ANTIMONY (Sb), BISMUTH (Bi).

EXPERIMENT 122.

Object. — *To obtain clear solutions of compounds of these metals, for use in the study of their reactions.*

Manipulation and Notes. — Put 20 cc. of water into each of three tubes. Into one, *a*, put a few small granules of arsenious oxide ($As_2 O_3$), and heat (*note*). Into a second, *b*, put a few drops of antimony chloride ($Sb Cl_3$) (*note*). Into the third, *c*, put a few grains of bismuth nitrate ($Bi (NO_3)_2$) (*note*).

Next add H Cl, drop by drop, to each (*note*). Which compound is soluble in water? Which are decomposed by water? Which are soluble in acid water?

EXPERIMENT 123.

Object. — *To precipitate and study the properties of the sulphides of these metals.*

1. To Precipitate the Sulphides.

Manipulation and Notes. — Proceed with the solutions just obtained (Exp. 122), treating each separately with $H_2 S$, as in previous cases. To save time, study the character of one of the sulphides while another is being precipitated (*note*).

2. To Study the Characters of these Sulphides.

Manipulation and Notes. — Follow the plan outlined for the study of tin sulphide (Exp. 120, 2). The results may be written out for each separately, as usual; or they may be tabulated as follows. Prepare a skeleton table as shown, and fill in the facts, stated in brief, when discovered.

Comparison of Sulphides of As, Sb, Bi.

SULPHIDES.	COLOR.	IN H Cl	IN HNO₃	IN (NH₄)₂ S
$As_2 S_3$				
$Sb_2 S_3$				
$Bi_2 S_3$				

Put the formulas of the tin sulphides in the table, below $Bi_2 S_3$; fill the blanks opposite; compare these sulphides with those of arsenic, antimony, and bismuth, and note the resemblances and differences.

General. — The foregoing work should have revealed the close general resemblance between the compounds of As, Sb, and Bi, and of their reactions; also some marked differences in details. By these differences you would be able to distinguish one from another (*explain*).

EXPERIMENT 124.

Object. — *To study the action of nascent hydrogen on arsenic trioxide.*

Manipulation and Notes. — To liberate the H, put pure zinc and water into a bottle generator (Fig. 13, p. 23). To dry the gas produced, attach a calcium chloride tube to the delivery tube of the bottle, and to this attach a hard glass tube drawn to a small opening at the other end. Pour dilute sulphuric acid into the bottle until effervescence occurs. *Let the gas drive all the air out of the apparatus.* Then fire the jet of H, and observe the flame (*note*). Pour a very little solution of arsenic trioxide in dilute hydrochloric acid into the bottle. Observe the flame (*note*). If it is a flame of H, then water is the only product; but hold a cold piece of white porcelain across its tip (*note*). The deposit is arsenic. Hence the burning gas must be the compound of arsenic and hydrogen (As H_3) produced by the action of nascent H on the As_2O_3. This is a delicate test for arsenic (Marsh's).

C. Exercise in Collecting and Tabulating Results of Experiments.

Object. — *To compare the sulphides of mercury, copper, lead, cadmium, zinc, tin, and bismuth.*

Prepare a skeleton table like that below. Fill the blanks by consulting your notes as directed in Exercise **A**, p. 94.

Table: Comparison of Properties of some Sulphides.

METALS.	SUL- PHIDES.	COLOR.	SOL'Y IN H_2O	SOL'Y IN HNO_3	SOL'Y IN H Cl	SOL'Y IN $(NH_4)_2 S$
Hg	Hg S					
Cu						
Pb						
Cd						
Zn						
Bi						
Sn^{ous}						
Sn^{ic}						

In what respect does the Zn S differ from all the others? In what respect do the tin sulphides differ from the others?

8

XII. ALUMINUM (Al).

EXPERIMENT 125.

Object. — To ascertain whether an aluminum compound in solution will be changed to a chloride by hydrochloric acid.

Manipulation and Notes. — Prepare 20 to 30 cc. of solution of alum $(K_2 Al_2 (SO_4)_4 + 24 H_2 O)$. Add HCl until the acid is in excess (*explain*). Then evaporate the solution to crystallization. Pour the liquid away, and rinse the crystals with water to remove all trace of HCl. Compare the product with the alum. Is any chemical change visible ?

You can decide whether the product is still a sulphate by treating its solution with drops of HCl followed by $BaCl_2$ (Exp. 48); or whether it is a chloride, by $AgNO_3$ followed by $NH_4 OH$ (Exp. 38). Note your conclusion.

The use of other soluble compounds of Al would lead to the same conclusion.

EXPERIMENT 126.

Object. — To ascertain whether an aluminum compound in solution will be changed by ammonium hydroxide.

Manipulation and Notes. — Make a dilute solution of alum in $H_2 O$, and add $NH_4 OH$ little by little to excess (*note*). Aluminum hydroxide $(Al_2 (HO)_6)$ is white; as a precipitate, it is gelatinous. Is it insoluble in water ? If so, it must have appeared with the addition of the first drops of NH_4OH. Is it insoluble in cold NH_4OH? If so, it did not disappear when NH_4OH was added in excess. Is it soluble in HCl? Try it (*note*). Is it soluble in KOH? Try it (*note*).

EXPERIMENT 127.

Object. — *To learn whether an aluminum compound in solution is affected by sodium hydroxide.*

Manipulation and Notes. — To a dilute solution of alum in water add, drop by drop, a dilute solution of sodium hydroxide (*note*). Add the hydroxide to excess (*note*). Can you explain the changes? How does this action of the $NaOH$ differ from that of NH_4OH (Exp. 126)?

EXPERIMENT 128.

Object. — *To learn the effect of heat on alum.*

Manipulation and Notes. — Put a few crystals of alum that seem to be dry into a dry tube, and heat them slowly (*note*). What seems to condense in the upper part of the tube? Continue the heat (*note*). Can you boil the alum all away? That which escaped was water, which is a necessary constituent of the crystals. It is called *water of crystallization.*

Use gypsum. See if you can detect its water of crystallization. If you can drive it all off, you will obtain plaster of Paris.

Some substances lose their water of crystallization on exposure to air. Try bright crystals of sodium sulphate. This change is called *efflorescence.*

XIII. CHROMIUM (Cr).

EXPERIMENT 129.

Object. — *To observe the change which may occur when a soluble chromium salt is treated with an alkaline hydroxide.*

Manipulation and Notes. — (*a*) Use the double sulphate of K and Cr ($KCr(SO_4)_2 + 12 H_2O$) known as chrome alum. Dissolve a small quantity in water, and add NH_4OH little by little (*note*) to excess (*note*). The visible product is $Cr_2(HO)_6$. Is it soluble in cold NH_4OH? Is it soluble in hot NH_4OH? Let there be large excess, and heat it just to boiling. Let the precipitate settle, and note the color of the liquid. Boil the liquid in a porcelain dish for several minutes (*note*).

(*b*) To another solution of the chrome alum add drops of KOH (*note*), then more KOH to excess (*note*). Compare the color of this solution with that obtained by NH_4OH.

Write the reaction for the $Cr_2(HO)_6$ in (*a*); also the reaction for the hydroxide in (*b*). Does the same hydroxide seem to be produced by the two alkalies?

General. — The different colors of the two solutions of the same hydroxide suggest that there are two forms or varieties of this hydroxide, — the violet and the green. In this respect the hydroxide in solution is typical of the chromium salts. There are two modifications, — the violet and the green.

(*c*) Is the $Cr_2(HO)_6$ soluble in NH_4Cl?

EXPERIMENT 130.

Object. — *To study the change which may occur when a soluble chromium salt is treated with* $(NH_4)_2 S$.

Manipulation and Notes. — Use the solution of a little chrome alum in water. Add the $(NH_4)_2 S$ little by little, to excess (*note*). Compare the precipitate with the hydroxide in Exp. 129 (*note*). Is it a sulphide or the hydroxide? Try to prove that it is not a sulphide (*explain*). Compare Exp. 128.

EXPERIMENT 131.

Object. — *To study the effect of a strong oxidizing agent on a solid chromium salt.*

Manipulation and Notes. — Use chrome alum, and oxidize it by fusion with KNO_3 as follows. Make a little mixture of powdered KNO_3 and powdered Na_2CO_3, and add a very little powdered chrome alum. Put the mixture on a piece of broken porcelain dish, or, better, platinum foil. Hold this support, with forceps, in the top of the Bunsen flame, and heat it gradually until the mixture melts. Keep it melted for some time, and then let it cool.

If the fusion has been successful, the color of the fused mass may give some evidence of chemical change (*note*). Boil the fused mass in a small quantity of water; filter the solution; and, if its color is not distinct, evaporate it down to smaller bulk. Does it seem to contain either the violet or green chromium salt? Test a little of it with NH_4OH (Exp. 129). Does it act like a chromium salt? Obtain a little solution of potassium chromate. Does your product resemble this?

General. — This experiment should illustrate the power of strong oxidizing agents to change Cr from the *basic* to the *acid* part of its salts. In chromium sulphate ($Cr_2(SO_4)_3$), Cr is the basic element; in potassium chromate (K_2CrO_4), potassium is the basic element, while chromium is in the acid radical. These two salts are types of two large classes of chromium compounds.

EXPERIMENT 132.

Object. — *To learn the effect, if any, of oxidizing agents on potassium chromate.*

Manipulation and Notes. — Make a solution of K_2CrO_4 in water. Divide it into two portions, and add HNO_3 to one (*note*). Judge by the color whether chemical change occurs. Then evaporate both solutions to crystallization. Compare the crystals. The new salt is potassium dichromate ($K_2Cr_2O_7$).

General. — These two potassium chromates are typical of two classes of chromates, — the yellow *normal chromates*, and the orange red *dichromates;* and the yellow salts are easily changed into the red by an oxidizing agent.

EXPERIMENT 133

Object. — *To observe the effect, if any, of hydrochloric acid and hydrogen sulphide on a solution of a dichromate.*

Manipulation and Notes. — Add a little HCl to a solution of $K_2Cr_2O_7$ (*note*). Heat the mixture to boiling (*note*). Then pass H_2S into the hot solution (*note*). You can judge by the color whether the liquid now contains the dichromate, a normal chromate, or a chromium salt.

$$K_2Cr_2O_7 + 8HCl + 3H_2S = 2KCl + 7H_2O + Cr_2Cl_6 + S_3.$$

Did you see any free S in the liquid? What became of the H of the H_2S?

General. — This experiment illustrates the fact that a dichromate is *reduced* to a Cr salt by the action of substances whose elements have strong affinity for O, as the H in H_2S has: in other words, by reducing agents.

EXPERIMENT 134.

Object. — *To observe the effect of ammonium sulphide on a dichromate.*

Manipulation and Notes. — To a solution of $K_2Cr_2O_7$ in a tube add a little $(NH_4)_2S$ (*note*). The change in color may help you to judge what change occurred in the dichromate.

EXPERIMENT 135.

Object. — *To become acquainted with the behavior of a solid compound of chromium when fused with borax.*

Manipulation and Notes. — Insert the platinum wire loop (Fig. 33, p. 85), when hot or moistened, into powdered borax, and fuse the adhering borax in the blowpipe or Bunsen flame. Repeat until the loop is filled with a transparent bead. Moisten the clear cold bead, and touch it to a very little of the powdered given solid. Now melt the substance into the bead by means of the outer or oxidizing blowpipe flame, and note the color of the bead while hot, and after it has become cold. Is the solid dissolved in the bead? Is the bead distinctly colored?

Fuse the bead, containing the substance, in the inner or reducing blowpipe flame (*note*).

XIV. MANGANESE (Mn).

EXPERIMENT 136.

Object. — *To study the change which may occur when a manganous salt is treated with an alkaline hydroxide.*

Manipulation and Notes. — (*a*) Use the manganous chloride ($MnCl_2$) or the manganous sulphate ($MnSO_4$). Dissolve in water, and treat the solution with NH_4OH, as in Exp. 129 (*a*) (*note*); and with KOH, as in Exp. 129 (*b*) (*note*). Note any change in the color of the product taking place at once or on standing.

(*b*) Will the action of the hydroxide NH_4OH be affected by the presence of NH_4Cl? Try it. Use large proportion of NH_4Cl. Let this mixture stand (*note*).

EXPERIMENT 137.

Object. — *To convert any soluble salt of manganese into the sulphide.*

Manipulation and Notes. — (*a*) Add $(NH_4)_2S$ little by little to a solution of the manganese salt (*note*). Study the reaction. Is the product a sulphide, or is it an hydroxide? Expose the freshly made product, on a filter, to the air for some time (*note*). Ascertain whether this sulphide is soluble in NH_4Cl.

General. — The foregoing experiments reveal the behavior of manganous compounds toward the reagents used, and, by comparison, the general resemblance of Mn to Cr in these reactions (*explain*). The special differences, also, are apparent (*explain*).

They also reveal the fact that the manganous hydroxide and sulphide change color on exposure to air. This is true of a few other manganous compounds. They are oxidized by the air. $Mn(OH)_2$ is oxidized to $Mn_2(OH)_6$; and this manganic hydroxide is the type of a class, — the manganic compounds.

EXPERIMENT 138.

Object. — *To study the effect of more energetic oxidizing agents on manganous compounds.*

Manipulation and Notes. — Reduce the compound (say dry $Mn(HO)_2$) to a fine powder, and use KNO_3 as the oxidizing agent. Proceed as directed in Exp. 131 to oxidize by fusion with KNO_3 and Na_2CO_3. Use the greatest heat you can command, but do not let the flame itself touch the mixture. (Hot illuminating gas is a reducing agent.) The tip of a blowpipe flame against the under surface of platinum foil may be used in preference to the Bunsen flame. Note the change in color which betrays the oxidation. If the color is not the same as that already obtained by oxidation in Exp. 137, it suggests a different product (*note*). Dissolve when cold in a small quantity of cold water, and filter the solution (*note*). Keep it.

General. — In this experiment you produce potassium manganate (K_2MnO_4). Manganese is no longer the basic element : it has become acidic. Compare with oxidation of chromium, Exp. 131. In the same way other manganous salts are changed to manganates.

EXPERIMENT 139.

Object. — *To ascertain whether potassium manganate, like potassium chromate, may be oxidized still further.*

Manipulation and Notes. — Use the solution obtained in the preceding experiment, or, better, a larger quantity made by dissolving the salt in water. Boil this solution (*note*). The change in color betrays the oxidation of K_2MnO_4 to $K_2Mn_2O_8$ (potassium permanganate).

$$3\,K_2MnO_4 + 2\,H_2O = K_2Mn_2O_8 + MnO_2 + 4\,KOH.$$

What is the oxidizing agent in this case?

EXPERIMENT 140.

Object. — *To ascertain whether potassium permanganate is easily reduced, and, if so, to what condition.*

Manipulation and Notes. — (*a*) To 10 cc. of water add potassium permanganate enough to color it very distinctly, then a little KOH, and boil the mixture (*note*). Judge by the color what compound is formed by the reduction of $K_2Mn_2O_8$.

(*b*) To a very dilute solution of $K_2Mn_2O_8$, first add a little sugar, then KOH, and boil the mixture (*note*). To what condition is the $K_2Mn_2O_8$ now reduced?

(*c*) Put a little sugar alone with the dilute $K_2Mn_2O_8$, and boil it more persistently (*note*).

General. — The sugar represents other substances whose elements have strong attraction for oxygen. By these the $K_2Mn_2O_8$ is reduced beyond the green K_2MnO_4 to lower compounds, which are brown.

EXPERIMENT 141.

Object. — *To become acquainted with the behavior of manganese compounds in the "borax bead."*

Manipulation and Notes. — Proceed as with Cr in Exp. 135.

XV. IRON (Fe).

EXPERIMENT 142.

Object. — *To study the reactions of ferrous and ferric compounds with an alkaline hydroxide.*

Manipulation and Notes. — Prepare two tubes, — one with a dilute solution of ferrous chloride ($FeCl_2$), the other with a dilute solution of ferric chloride (Fe_2Cl_6). To the first add a little NH_4OH (*note*), then to excess (*note*). Treat the second in the same way. Pour the first upon a filter to be examined afterward.

Write and explain the reaction in each case. Mark the differences of the two hydroxides in appearance and composition. They are typical differences of the ferrous and ferric compounds generally.

Examine the hydroxide left on the filter (*note*). Explain the change. Ascertain whether NH_4Cl will prevent the precipitation of these hydroxides.

EXPERIMENT 143.

Object. — *To study the reaction of soluble iron compounds with ammonium sulphide.*

Manipulation and Notes. — Prepare two tubes, — one with a dilute solution of ferrous chloride, the other with a dilute solution of ferric chloride. To the first add drops of $(NH_4)_2S$ (*note*). Treat the second in the same way. Judging by appearances, are the two precipitates the same, or different substances? Can you write the two reactions on the hypothesis that the two are the same substance? Ascertain whether this sulphide is soluble in HCl.

EXPERIMENT 144.

Object. — *To study the effect of oxidizing agents on ferrous compounds.*

Manipulation and Notes. — (*a*) Use HNO_3. To about 5 cc. of water add about 1 cc. of solution of $FeCl_2$ and 4 or 5 drops of HNO_3. Boil the mixture gently for about a minute. The change in color should indicate the change in composition, and by drops of NH_4OH (as in Exp. 142) you can decide whether that change has occurred.

(*b*) Use $K_2Mn_2O_8$. Acidulate a solution of ferrous chloride. Add $K_2Mn_2O_8$ (*note*) until its color can be just detected in the liquid (*give reason*). Some indication of a change in the $FeCl_2$ should have been observed during the work. Can you prove that the $FeCl_2$ has been changed to Fe_2Cl_6?

EXPERIMENT 145.

Object. — *To study the action of reducing agents on ferric compounds.*

Manipulation and Notes. — (*a*) Use H_2S. Acidulate a solution of ferric chloride with HCl. Then pass H_2S gas through it (*note*). A change in color should suggest the chemical change. Can you prove that the iron has been reduced to ferrous form?

Write the reaction and explain it.

(*b*) Use nascent hydrogen. The H may be liberated by zinc and sulphuric acid. The better way is to use amalgamated zinc with a strip of platinum. Thus: Clean a few pieces of granulated zinc by immersion in dilute H_2SO_4. Amalgamate them by contact with mercury. Place them in a test tube, and put a piece of platinum in contact with them. Prepare a dilute solution of ferrous sulphate, its color visible. Add some dilute H_2SO_4 and pour it upon the Zn. Close the tube with a stopper having a small hole for escape of gas, to cut off free access of air (*give reason*), and let the whole stand (*note*). Finally you can decide by color (*explain*) and test (*explain*) whether the iron remains in the ferric or the ferrous form. Write and explain the reaction.

EXPERIMENT 146.

Object. — *To become acquainted with another test by which to decide whether a solution contains a ferrous or a ferric compound.*

Manipulation and Notes. — Try to convert the iron into " Prussian blue " by means of potassium ferrocyanide. Prepare two tubes, — one with a dilute solution of a ferric salt, the other with a dilute solution of a ferrous salt. Acidulate each with a drop or two of H Cl. To the first add drops of potassium ferrocyanide (*note*). Treat the second in the same way (*note*). Mark the difference in the products. The first is the " Prussian blue."

EXPERIMENT 147.

Object. — *To become acquainted with the behavior of iron compounds in the " borax bead."*

Manipulation and Notes. — Proceed as directed in Exp. 135.

D. Exercise in Collecting and Tabulating Results of Experiments.

Object. — *To compare the properties of the hydroxides of zinc, aluminum, chromium, manganese, iron.*

Prepare a skeleton table like that on p. 126. Fill the blanks by gleaning the facts from your own notes, as directed in Exercise **A**, p. 94.

Table: Comparison of Properties of some Hydroxides.

METALS.	HYDROXIDES.	COLOR.	SOL'Y IN NH_4OH	SOL'Y IN NH_4Cl
Zn				
Al				
Cr				
Mn				
Fe^{ous}				
Fe^{ic}				

A given solution contains a compound of either Zn or Al: how would you decide which?

A solution contains a compound of either Mn or Fe: how would you decide which? In what respect does the Mn hydroxide differ from the Zn hydroxide?

A solution contains a compound of iron: how would you decide whether it is a ferrous or a ferric compound?

XVI. NICKEL (Ni), COBALT (Co).

EXPERIMENT 148.

Object. — *To study the reactions of soluble nickel and cobalt compounds with an alkaline hydroxide, and to compare the two hydroxides.*

Manipulation and Notes. — (*a*) To a dilute solution of the given salt (use the sulphate) add NH_4OH gradually (*note*) to excess (*note*). Compare the reactions and results obtained with Ni and Co compounds. Ascertain whether the hydroxide is soluble in NH_4Cl.

(*b*) Use KOH instead of NH_4OH in the same way. Note carefully any differences in the results with compounds of Ni and Co. Note also any differences in the action of the two alkaline hydroxides used. Also compare the hydroxides of Ni and Co with those of Fe, Mn, Cr, and Zn.

EXPERIMENT 149.

Object. — *To convert soluble compounds of nickel and cobalt into sulphides, and to compare the products.*

Manipulation and Notes. — Add $(NH_4)_2S$ to a dilute solution of the given substance (*note*). Compare these two sulphides, and the reactions which produced them. Ascertain whether these sulphides are soluble in HCl.

General. — The foregoing experiments should reveal the very close resemblance of compounds of Ni and Co, in their behavior toward the reagents used. This resemblance is maintained throughout all the chemical relations of these two metals.

EXPERIMENT 150.

Object. — *To become acquainted with the potassium-cyanide test, by which to decide whether a given solution contains a nickel or a cobalt compound.*

Manipulation and Notes. — (*a*) Make a fresh solution of potassium cyanide (K Cy) in water. Add this in *small quantity* to the given solution (*note*). Then add more of the K Cy, but no more than needed to complete the change (*note*). Finally add H Cl (*note*). Use the Ni and Co sulphates.

(*b*) Acidify the given solution with several drops of acetic acid. Add the K Cy as in (*a*), shaking the liquid. Boil the solution for some time; let it cool; and finally add H Cl in excess, and let the mixture stand for some time. Use the Ni and Co sulphates.

EXPERIMENT 151.

Object. — *To become acquainted with the behavior of compounds of nickel and cobalt in the "borax bead."*

Manipulation and Notes. — Proceed as directed in Exp. 135.

E. Exercise in Collecting and Tabulating Results of Experiments.

Object. — *To compare the properties of the sulphides of zinc, manganese, iron, nickel, cobalt, copper, tin.*

Prepare a skeleton table like that on p. 129. Fill the blanks by gleaning the facts from your own notes, as di rected in Exercise **A,** p. 94.

Table: Comparison of Properties of some Sulphides.

METALS.	SULPHIDES.	COLOR.	SOL'Y IN HNO$_3$	SOL'Y IN HCl	SOL'Y IN (NH$_4$)$_2$S
Zn					
Mn					
Fe					
Ni					
Co					
Cu					
Sn					

In what respect do the first five sulphides in this table differ from the last two?

If a solution should contain all these metals in the form of chlorides, by what reagent would you precipitate them all in the form of sulphides? Having the mixture of all these sulphides, by what solvent could you separate the first five from the last two? Having the last two only, how could you separate them?

9

PART III.

APPLICATION OF CERTAIN FOREGOING REACTIONS TO QUALITATIVE ANALYSIS.

I. PRELIMINARY STATEMENTS.

THE foregoing study of the chemical characters of elements and compounds has shown that each differs from every other in some particulars, but that in other respects several may be much alike.

By the general *resemblances* between certain of their compounds, the metals may all be placed in a few groups. By the specific *differences* of these same or other compounds, the individual metals in a group may be identified.

This application of our knowledge of general chemistry to determine the constituents of substances whose composition is unknown to us is of the highest practical value.

You should now try to collect and classify the facts which you have discovered in order that you may use them for this purpose; that is, for the purpose of *Qualitative Analysis.*

II. THE ANALYTICAL CLASSIFICATION.

The *grouping* of the metals *is founded upon the solubility* of a few classes of their compounds.

For example: You found that silver chloride is insoluble in water (Exp. 105), and that copper chloride is soluble in water (Exp. 108). For this reason silver chloride can be precipitated by HCl, while copper chloride cannot be.

Now, *all* metals *whose chlorides are*, like that of silver, *insoluble in water*, may be put with silver to form one group. In the same way, metals whose sulphides are insoluble may form another group; and so on for others.

But you have examined the solubility of a large number of compounds, and the facts are in your note-book. If you will collect and tabulate them, you will have the analytical classification as a result of your own investigation.

Proceed as follows: Prepare a skeleton table with six columns, like that below, and fill the blanks by gleaning the facts from your own notes. In each column write the symbols of the metals whose *compounds* are insoluble as described at the head of the column; but omit from each column those already placed in the columns before it.

III. THE ANALYTICAL GROUPS.

CHLORIDES INSOLUBLE IN H_2O AND HCl	SULPHIDES INSOLUBLE IN H_2O AND HCl	HYDROXIDES INSOLUBLE IN NH_4OH AND NH_4Cl	SULPHIDES SOLUBLE IN HCl. INSOL. IN NH_4OH	CARBONATES INSOLUBLE IN NH_4Cl AND NH_4OH	FOREGOING COMPOUNDS ALL SOLUBLE IN H_2O.
1....	1....	1....	1....	1....	1....
2....	2....	2....	2....	2....	2....
3....	3....	3....	3....	3....	3....
	4....		4....		4....
	5....				
	6....				
	7....				
GROUP I. Precipitated by HCl	GROUP II. Precipitated by H_2S	GROUP III. Precipitated by NH_4OH	GROUP IV. Precipitated by $(NH_4)_2S$	GROUP V. Precipitated by $(NH_4)_2CO_3$	GROUP VI. not Precipitated

IV. ANALYSIS OF A SIMPLE SALT.

1. To Find what Metal the Salt Contains.

If the salt is in the solid form, you first dissolve it. For the present we will suppose that it is soluble in water.

(*a*) *Is this salt a compound of a metal in Group I.?* To answer this question, try to convert it into a chloride. Put a small portion of the *strong* solution into a tube, and add H Cl drop by drop. If a *precipitate* is made, it must be a chloride of Ag, Hg_2, or Pb, — the metals of Group I., — since these are the only chlorides insoluble in H_2O and H Cl; and you can decide which it is by the different behavior of these chlorides toward hot water, ammonium hydroxide, and light, as discovered by experiments made in the study of these metals.

But if H Cl yields no precipitate, you judge that the salt is not a compound of Ag, Pb, or Hg_2.

(*b*) *Is the salt a compound of any metal in Group II.?* To answer this question, try to convert it into a sulphide. Treat a portion of the *diluted* solution, which has been made acid by drops of H Cl, with H_2S. If a precipitate is made, it must be a sulphide of Hg, Cd, Cu, Bi, As, Sb, or Sn (*give reason*). Proceed to ascertain which one by testing it for the properties in which those sulphides *differ*.

You have learned that the As, Sb, and Sn sulphides are soluble in $(NH_4)_2S$ (Exps. 123, 2; and 120, 2, *d*), while the other four sulphides are not. Hence proceed as directed in Exp. 123, 2 (*a*), (*d*), and you can decide whether the metal of the salt is one of the three, As, Sb, Sn; or one of the four, Hg, Cd, Bi, Cu.

Having decided this, you can proceed to identify the metal by experiments which you made in the study of these metals.

But if H_2S yields no precipitate, you are ready to declare that the salt is not a compound of any one of these seven metals (*give reason*).

(*c*) *Is the salt a compound of any metal in Group III.?* To answer this, try to convert it into an hydroxide. Use a portion of the original solution. Add considerable NH_4Cl,[1] and then add NH_4OH by drops until the liquid smells *strongly* of this substance.[1] Do not mistake the odor of the air above the liquid for that of the liquid. If a precipitate is made in this way, it must be an hydroxide of Cr, Al, or Fe (*give reason*); and you ascertain which one by experiments which you made when studying the character of these metals.

But if no precipitate is obtained by NH_4OH, you infer that the salt is not a compound of any one of these metals.

(*d*) *Is the salt a compound of any metal in Group IV.?* To answer this, try to convert it into a sulphide in presence of NH_4OH. For this purpose you can use the solution already in hand, containing NH_4Cl and NH_4OH, or you can add these reagents to a portion of the original solution.

Add $(NH_4)_2S$. If a precipitate appears, it must be a sulphide of Zn, Mn, Ni, or Co (*give reason*), and you can decide which by noting the *differences* in these sulphides and by experiments made in the study of these metals.

But the absence of a precipitate is evidence that the salt is not a compound of any one of these metals.

(*e*) *Is this salt a compound of any metal in Group V.?* To decide this question, try to convert it into a carbonate. Use a portion of the original solution. Add considerable NH_4Cl (*give reason*), and then $(NH_4)_2CO_3$. If a precipitate appears, it must be a carbonate of Ba, Sr, or Ca (*give rea-*

---

[1] For the object of adding NH_4Cl here and in future operations, see Exp. 92 (*c*); and Exp. 136 (*b*). For the object of using "excess" of NH_4OH, see Exp. 96.

son), and you can decide which one by the differences in their reactions discovered by Exp. 93 (*a*) and (*b*).

But if no precipitate appears, no compound of any one of these metals can be present, and you must conclude that the salt is a compound of one of the metals in Group VI.

(*f*) Which one of the four ? To ascertain which, you may make Exps. 88 and 89.

2. To Find what Acid Radical the Salt Contains.

The next object is to learn whether the salt is a chloride, a nitrate, or some other compound of the metal. But the characteristic reactions of these classes of salts have been revealed by your study of them in Part I. Thus, you can identify a chloride by Exp. 38; a sulphate, by Exp. 48; a nitrate, by Exp. 67; a carbonate, by Exp. 72; and others, by experiments made in the course of your work.

Having found the metal in the salt, and its acid radical, you can announce the name of the substance.

For practice in the analysis of simple salts, you should receive substances from the instructor. Follow the foregoing *general* directions, but at the same time consult a good book on *qualitative analysis* for information which the foregoing studies have not been carried far enough to impart.

3. Hints in Regard to Notes.

In this work your notes should be kept faithfully and systematically. They should contain a brief account of every step and the inference drawn from it. Every step that goes wrong, no less than those which seem to go right, should be recorded, with the cause of the failure, if you can discover it. Never discard an experiment nor "begin over" unless you can give a good reason for doing so. At the end of the analysis, your notes should be handed to the teacher as your "Report" on the work.

One good form in which to keep these notes is given below. It is the "three-column" system. Do not forget to head the sheet with your name, the date, and the designation of the substance, as shown.

Name... *Date* ....

Substance No.................

EXPERIMENTS.	RESULTS.	INFERENCES.
I. Add drops of H Cl.	No precipitate made.	Absence of Group I. Ag, Hg (ous), Pb.
II. To I. add H₂ S.	No precipitate made.	Absence of Group II. Hg (ic), Bi, Cu, Cd, As, Sb, Sn.
III. To the original solution add NH₄Cl and NH₄OH.	No precipitate made.	Absence of Group III. Fe, Al, Cr.
IV. To III. add (NH₄)₂ S.	No precipitate made.	Absence of Group IV. Mn, Zn, Ni, Co.
V. To original solution add NH₄Cl and (NH₄)₂ C O₃.	A white precipitate.	Presence of Group V. Ba, Sr, or Ca.
VI. To the original solution add solution of Ca S O₄.	No precipitate made in the cold.	Absence of Ba.
VII. Heat VI. to boiling.	A white precipitate.	Presence of Sr.
VIII. Flame test.	Brilliant crimson.	Confirms presence of Sr.

Hence substance No........... is a compound of strontium.

V. ANALYSIS OF A COMPLEX SUBSTANCE.

A substance which contains more than one metal or salt may be analyzed by a skillful use of the foregoing facts. If, for example, you have a mixture of silver nitrate and copper nitrate, you can *separate* the two metals, and then identify each; for, if you add HCl to the solution of the mixture, you will convert the Ag into white insoluble AgCl, while the copper compound will stay in solution. If, then, you filter the mixture, you will have the silver in the precipitate on the filter, and the copper in the filtrate. You can prove the white precipitate to be silver chloride, and thus *prove* that Ag was present in the original substance; and you can also identify Cu in the filtrate, and thus prove that this metal was also present in the original substance.

Thus, "separations" of the metals belonging to different groups can be made by the use of the group reagents HCl, H_2S, and so on, in their proper order, and then the metals in each group may be identified.

But the full directions for such advanced work would better be obtained from the instructor, or found in works devoted to *Qualitative Analysis*.

APPENDIX.

A. The Names, Symbols, and Approximate Atomic Masses (Atomic Weights) of the Elements.

NAMES.	Symbols.	Atomic Masses.	NAMES.	Symbols.	Atomic Masses.
Aluminum . . .	Al.	27	Molybdenum .	Mo.	96
Antimony . . .	Sb.	120	Nickel	Ni.	58.5
Arsenic	As.	75	Nitrogen	N.	14
Barium	Ba.	137	Osmium	Os.	191
Beryllium[1] . . .	Be.	9	Oxygen . . .	O.	16
Bismuth	Bi.	207	Palladium . . .	Pd.	106
Boron	B.	11	Phosphorus . .	P.	31
Bromine	Br.	80	Platinum . . .	Pt.	194
Cadmium	Cd.	112	Potassium . . .	K.	39
Cæsium	Cs.	133	Rhodium . . .	Rh.	104
Calcium	Ca.	40	Rubidium . . .	Rb.	85
Carbon	C.	12	Ruthenium . .	Ru.	103.5
Cerium	Ce.	141	Samarium . . .	Sm.	150
Chlorine	Cl.	35.5	Scandium . . .	Sc.	44
Chromium . . .	Cr.	52	Selenium . . .	Se.	79
Cobalt	Co.	59	Silicon	Si.	28
Columbium[2] . .	Cb.	94	Silver	Ag.	108
Copper	Cu.	63.3	Sodium	Na.	23
Didymium . . .	Di.	142	Strontium . . .	Sr.	87.3
Erbium	Er.	166	Sulphur	S.	32
Fluorine	F.	19	Tantalum . . .	Ta.	182
Gallium	Ga.	70	Tellurium . . .	Te.	125
Germanium . .	Gr.	73	Terbium	Tb.	148
Gold	Au.	196.7	Thallium . . .	Tl.	204
Hydrogen	H.	1	Thorium	Th.	232
Indium	In.	113.4	Tin	Sn.	118
Iodine	I.	127	Titanium . . .	Ti.	48
Iridium	Ir.	193	Tungsten[3] . . .	W.	184
Iron	Fe.	56	Uranium	U.	240
Lanthanum . . .	La.	138.5	Vanadium . . .	V.	51.2
Lead	Pb.	207	Ytterbium . . .	Yb.	173
Lithium	Li.	7	Yttrium	Yt.	89
Magnesium . . .	Mg.	24	Zinc	Zn.	65
Manganese . . .	Mn.	55	Zirconium . . .	Zr.	90
Mercury	Hg.	200			

[1] Beryllium is also called glucinum, with the symbol Gl.
[2] Columbium is also called niobium, with the symbol Nb.
[3] Tungsten has also been called Wolframium.

B. The Metric Measures, with their Equivalent English Values.

1. Measures of Length.

The standard unit is the meter, — the length, at 0° C., of a certain bar of platinum preserved in the Archives, Paris.

	1 millimeter (mm.)	=	0.03937	inch.
10 millimeters	= 1 centimeter (cm.)	=	0.3937	"
10 centimeters	= 1 decimeter (dm.)	=	3.9371	inches.
10 decimeters	= 1 METER (m.)	=	39.3707	"
10 meters	= 1 decameter (dcm.)	=	32.81	feet.
10 decameters	= 1 hectometer (hm.)	=	109.36	yards.
10 hectometers	= 1 kilometer (km.)	=	0.6214	mile.

1 meter = 3.2809 feet = 1.0936 yards.

1 inch = 2.534 centimeters.   1 foot = 30.479 centimeters.

1 yard = 0.9144 meter.   1 mile = 1.6093 kilometers.

2. Measures of Volume or Capacity.

The unit is the liter, — the volume of pure water which at 4° C. would just fill a cubical vessel, each of whose sides is one decimeter in length.

1 cubic centimeter (cc.)	= 1 milliliter	= 0.06103	cubic inch.
10 cc. = 10 milliliters	= 1 centiliter	= 0.6103	" "
100 cc. = 10 centiliters	= 1 deciliter	= 6.1027	cubic inches.
1000 cc. = 10 deciliters	= 1 LITER (l.)	= 1.0567	U. S. quarts.

0.9469 liters = 1 U. S. liq. quart = 57.752 cubic inches.

3.785 liters = 1 U. S. gallon = 231   "   "

4.544 liters = 1 Imp. gallon = 277.27   "   "

29.57 cubic centimeters = 1 U. S. fluid ounce = $1\frac{1}{16}$ U. S. pint.

28.4 cubic centimeters = 1 Imp. fluid ounce = $\frac{1}{20}$ Imp. pint.

16.386 cubic centimeters = 1 cubic inch = 0.554 U. S. quart.

3. Measures of Mass or Relative Weight.

The standard unit is the kilogram, — the mass of a certain block of platinum preserved in the Archives, Paris. The smaller unit, one gram, is the weight of one cubic centimeter of pure water at 4° C.

	1 milligram (mg.) =	0.0154	grain.
10 milligrams	= 1 centigram (cg.) =	0.1543	"
10 centigrams	= 1 decigram (dg.) =	1.5432	grains.
10 decigrams	= 1 GRAM (g.) =	15.4323	"
10 grams	= 1 decagram (dcg.) =	154.323	"
10 decagrams	= 1 hectogram (hg.) =	3.527	ozs. Avoir.
10 hectograms	= 1 kilogram (kg.) =	2.2046	lbs. Avoir.

0.4535 kilograms = 1 lb. Avoir. 28.349 grams = 1 oz. Avoir.
0.3872 kilograms = 1 lb. Troy. 31.103 grams = 1 oz. Troy.

4. MEASURES OF TEMPERATURE.

Freezing point of water =   0° Centigrade (C.) or 32° Fahrenheit (F).
Boiling point of water = 100°   "   or 212°   "

$$1° C. = \tfrac{9}{5}° \text{ or } 1.8° F. \qquad 1° F. = \tfrac{5}{9}° \text{ or } 0.555° C.$$

To change a Centigrade temperature to its equivalent Fahrenheit temperature, multiply by $\tfrac{9}{5}$, and add 32° to the product.

To change a Fahrenheit temperature to its equivalent Centigrade temperature, subtract 32, and multiply the remainder by $\tfrac{5}{9}$.

C. Apparatus and Chemicals.

1. THE APPARATUS.

The following list includes all the apparatus required for the experimental course described in this book. The set has been arranged with special reference to the needs of beginners, and to the wants of teachers who are oftentimes so pressed by other duties that little time is left for the preparation and oversight of laboratory work.

Many of these articles, once obtained, should last a long time; many others are more likely to perish, and should be bought in larger number than that prefixed to them in the list, which indicates the outfit for a single table. Further suggestions on this point may be found in the notes which follow the list.

1 Balance.

BEAKERS, Griffin's low, wide, with lip:—
2   No. 00, capacity 1½ ounces.
1   " 0,   "   2½   "
1   " 1,   "   5   "

1 Blowpipe, jeweler's, brass, 10 inches.

BOTTLES, wide-mouthed, flint glass, round: ——
2   Capacity 4 ounces.
2   "   6   "
2   "   8   "

1 Bunsen burner, with regulator for air.
2 Burettes, Mohr's, with tip for pinchcock.
1 Chloride-of-calcium tube (drying tube) 1 bulb, 6 inches.
1 Cobalt glass, plate 2×3 inches.
1 Cork borers, set of 3, for holes, $\frac{2}{16}$, $\frac{3}{16}$, $\frac{4}{16}$ inch.
1 File, triangular, 5 inches.

FLASKS: ——
4   Erlenmeyer form (conical), Bohemian glass, ring-neck, diame-
    ter of mouth 1 inch, capacity 10 ounces.
1   Round-bottom, ring-neck, diameter of mouth $\frac{3}{4}$ inch, capacity
    8 ounces.
1   Side-neck, tube set high, capacity 5 ounces, diameter of mouth
    $\frac{3}{4}$ inch.
1   Side-neck, tube set high, capacity 8 ounces, diameter of mouth
    $\frac{3}{4}$ inch.

1 Forceps (pincers), steel, plain, $4\frac{1}{2}$ inches.
1 Funnel, best German, 60°, stem pointed, diameter $2\frac{1}{2}$ inches.
1 Funnel tube, thistle top, 10 inches.
2 Glass stirrers (rods), one end rounded, 8 inches.
1 pound glass tubing, best German, $\frac{3}{16}$ inch outside diameter.
1 Graduated cylinder, on foot, 25cc. with lip.
1 Mortar, of German porcelain, deep form, with pestle, diameter
    $3\frac{1}{2}$ inches.
2 Pinchcocks, Mohr's, medium size, strong spring.
1 Platinum foil, medium thick, for blowpiping, $1\frac{1}{2}$ inches square.
1 Platinum wire, No. 26, 3 inches.

PORCELAIN DISHES, Royal Berlin, glazed inside and outside: ——
2   No. 00, diameter $2\frac{1}{4}$ inches.
1   "   0,   "   3   "
1   "   3,   " $3\frac{1}{4}$ "

1 Retort stand, iron, 3 rings.
1 Retort-stand clamp, Bunsen's small universal, with **fastener**.

RUBBER STOPPERS, best soft rubber: ——
4   With 2 holes, selected to fit the conical flasks.
1   "   1 hole,   "   "   "   round-bottom **flask**.
2   "   1 hole,   "   "   "   side-neck **flasks**.

2   Solid, selected to fit the side-neck flasks.

1   Solid,   "   "   "   side-neck ignition tube.

3 feet rubber tubing, white, best quality, usual thickness, $\frac{3}{16}$ inch in diameter inside.

  Rubber tubing, for the Bunsen burner, $\frac{1}{4}$ inch inside, white, double thickness. (Length depends on the position of the gas fixture.)

1 Spatula, horn, 5 inches.

6 Test tubes, $6 \times \frac{5}{8}$ inches.

1 Test tube with side neck, hard glass, for ignition, $6 \times \frac{5}{8}$ inches.

1 Test-tube brush, brass-wire handle.

1 Test-tube rack for 6 tubes.

1 Thermometer, chemical, scale C.° on stem, to 200°.

1 Water pan, agate ware, flat bottom, about 10×4 inches.

1 Weights, 20 g. to 1 mg. in case.

Notes.

1. It will not be necessary to provide all the articles in this complete set for every member of a class. One balance and set of weights, one thermometer, two or three pieces of platinum foil, one graduated cylinder, two burettes, and one set of cork borers, may suffice for a class of ten to twenty students if necessary.

2. Owing to the fragile and perishable character of some articles, they should be purchased in larger numbers than the above list would indicate. Such, for example, as test tubes, flasks, beakers, and porcelain dishes, should be bought by the dozen or gross, and always more than sufficient to supply the students in the outset. Rubber tubing should be bought by "the piece," which is 12 feet.

3. A balance sensitive to 1 mg. inclosed in a glass case is desirable. One which is sensitive to 1 cg. is less costly, and fairly satisfactory for all the work described. With only a pair of "hand scales," costing much less than the balance, very good work can be done.

4. For some pieces of the apparatus, cheap substitutes may be found among articles of familiar use in the household. Such substitution should be made only by compulsion. Students in chemistry are as much entitled to know what chemical apparatus is, as they are to know what chemical methods and principles are. It is better to obtain apparatus from reliable dealers who will supply it from the same stock from which they supply chemists. If, in our list, any exceptions to this are warranted, they may be found in the

test-tube rack, which can be made in good style by any carpenter who consults Fig. 2, p. 12, and the test-tube brush, for which a rod of wood, with a piece of sponge wired upon the end, is a good equivalent.

5. Before purchasing the apparatus, its cost can be learned by sending the list to a dealer in chemical supplies, who will return a statement of his prices.

2. THE CHEMICALS.

In the following list are included the names and formulas of all the chemicals required for the course of studies laid down in this book. These substances should be of the best quality. Many should be "C. P.;" i. e., chemically pure. It is well to buy chemicals as you should buy apparatus, from well-known dealers in laboratory supplies.

Reagents, which are to be used by students, should be kept upon their tables in small bottles: liquids in glass-stoppered bottles holding about 125 cc. (or four oz.), and solids in salt-mouth bottles holding 2 oz. If substances are to be used by the teacher or are to remain in stock, they may, for the most part, be kept in the bottles in which they are bought. Every bottle should be distinctly and permanently labelled.

Unless economy must be rigidly practiced, the supply will not be limited to the substances in this list. Specimens, in great variety, are very desirable.

Acetic acid, pure	$HC_2H_3O_2.$
Alcohol	$C_2H_6O.$
Alum	$K_2Al_2(SO_4)_4 + 24H_2O.$
Ammonium carbonate, C. P.	$(NH_4)_2CO_3.$
Ammonium chloride, C. P.	$NH_4Cl.$
Ammonium hydroxide	$NH_4OH.$
Ammonium nitrate, cryst.	$NH_4NO_3.$
Ammonium sulphate	$(NH_4)_2SO_4.$
Animal charcoal, or boneblack	$C.$
Antimony chloride, sol. C. P.	$SbCl_3.$
Arsenious oxide	$As_2O_3.$
Barium chloride, C. P.	$BaCl_2.$
Barium nitrate, C. P.	$Ba(NO_3)_2.$
Bismuth nitrate, cryst. C. P.	$Bi(NO_3)_3.$
Cadmium chloride	$CdCl_2.$
Calcium chloride, cryst. C. P.	$CaCl_2.$

Calcium chloride, granulated.
Calcium oxide (quicklime) . . . . . $Ca O$.
Calcium sulphate, calcin. . . . . . $Ca SO_4$.
Chrome alum . . . . $K_2 Cr_2 (SO_4)_4 + 24 H_2 O$.
Cobalt sulphate . . . . $Co SO_4$.
Cochineal.
Copper filings, or clippings.
Copper wire, No. 24 and No. 16 . . . Cu.
Copper chloride . . . . $Cu Cl_2$.
Copper oxide . . . . $Cu O$.
Copper sulphate, C. P. . . . . . . $Cu SO_4$.
Corks, best velvet, diam. small end, 1, $1\frac{3}{8}$,
    $\frac{3}{4}$, $\frac{3}{4}$, $\frac{1}{2}$ inch, by the dozen.
Ferrous chloride . . . . $Fe Cl_2$.
Ferric chloride . . . . $Fe_2 Cl_6$.
Ferrous sulphate, pure . . . . . . $Fe SO_4$.
Ferrous sulphide, sticks . . . . . . $Fe S$.
Filter paper, best German, white, sheets 19×19 inches.
Hydrochloric acid, pure . . . . . . $H Cl$.
Iron filings, coarse.
Iron wire, No. 24.
Lead acetate . . . . $Pb (C_2 H_3 O_2)_2$.
Lead nitrate . . . . $Pb (NO_3)_2$.
Litmus, cubes.
Logwood, chips or extract.
Magnesium ribbon . . . . Mg.
Magnesium chloride, cryst. . . . . . $Mg Cl_2$.
Magnesium sulphate, C. P. . . . . . $Mg SO_4$.
Manganous chloride . . . . $Mn Cl_2$.
Manganese dioxide, powder . . . . $Mn O_2$.
Manganous sulphate . . . . $Mn SO_4$.
Marble . . . . $Ca CO_3$ (impure).
Mercury, redistilled . . . . Hg.
Mercuric chloride . . . . $Hg Cl_2$.
Mercuric oxide . . . . $Hg O$.
Nickel sulphate . . . . $Ni SO_4$.
Nitric acid . . . . $H NO_3$.
Phosphorus . . . . P.
Potassium . . . . K.
Potassium bromide, C. P. . . . . . $K Br$.
Potassium carbonate, C. P. . . . . . $K_2 CO_3$.

Potassium chlorate . . . . $K\,Cl\,O_3$.
Potassium chromate . . . . $K_2\,Cr\,O_4$.
Potassium cyanide . . . . $K\,Cy$.
Potassium dichromate . . . . $K_2\,Cr_2\,O_7$.
Potassium ferrocyanide . . . . . . $K_4\,Fe\,Cy_6$.
Potassium hydroxide, pure . . . . . $K\,O\,H$.
Potassium iodide . . . . $K\,I$.
Potassium manganate . . . . $K_2\,Mn\,O_4$.
Potassium nitrate, cryst. . . . . . . $K\,N\,O_3$.
Potassium permanganate . . . . . . $K_2\,Mn_2\,O_8$.
Potassium sulphate, cryst. . . . . . $K_2\,S\,O_4$.
Silver nitrate, cryst. . . . . $Ag\,N\,O_3$.
Sodium . . . . Na.
Sodium biborate (borax) . . . . . . $Na_2\,B_4\,O_7 + 10\,H_2\,O$.
Sodium bromide . . . . $Na\,Br$.
Sodium bicarbonate . . . . $H\,Na\,C\,O_3$.
Sodium carbonate, C. P. . . . . . . $Na_2\,C\,O_3$.
Sodium chloride (common salt) . . . $Na\,Cl$.
Sodium hydroxide, C. P. . . . . . . $Na\,O\,H$.
Sodium nitrate . . . . $Na\,N\,O_3$.
Sodium sulphate . . . . $Na_2\,S\,O_4$.
Sodium sulphite . . . . $Na_2\,S\,O_3$.
Strontium chloride . . . . $Sr\,Cl_2$.
Strontium nitrate, C. P. . . . . . . $Sr\,(N\,O_3)_2$.
Sulphuric acid, pure . . . . $H_2\,S\,O_4$.
Sulphur, flowers . . . . S.
Sulphur, roll . . . . S.
Tin, granulated . . . . Sn.
Zinc, sheet, common . . . . Zn.
Zinc, granulated . . . . Zn.
Charcoal, common . . . . C.
Starch, common . . . . $C_6\,H_{10}\,O_5$.
Sugar, granulated, common . . . . . $C_{12}\,H_{22}\,O_{11}$.